The Happiest Book I Ever Read Is the Revelation of Jesus Christ

The Happiest Book I Ever Read Is the Revelation of Jesus Christ

Inductive Reading for Then and Now

WILMA ZALABAK

RESOURCE *Publications* • Eugene, Oregon

THE HAPPIEST BOOK I EVER READ IS THE REVELATION OF JESUS CHRIST
Inductive Reading for Then and Now

Copyright © 2022 Wilma Zalabak. All rights reserved. Except for brief quotations in critical publications or reviews, no part of this book may be reproduced in any manner without prior written permission from the publisher. Write: Permissions, Wipf and Stock Publishers, 199 W. 8th Ave., Suite 3, Eugene, OR 97401.

Resource Publications
An Imprint of Wipf and Stock Publishers
199 W. 8th Ave., Suite 3
Eugene, OR 97401

www.wipfandstock.com

PAPERBACK ISBN: 978-1-6667-5114-7
HARDCOVER ISBN: 978-1-6667-5115-4
EBOOK ISBN: 978-1-6667-5116-1

09/20/22

Scripture quotations from The Authorized (King James) Version. Rights in the Authorized Version in the United Kingdom are vested in the Crown. Reproduced by permission of the Crown's patentee, Cambridge University Press

Some Bible quotations are paraphrased from the KJV by Wilma Zalabak, and are so marked. The WZ paraphrase replaces "thee" and "thou" structures, inclusive male pronouns, and other formal-sounding words, like "shall." The WZ paraphrase removes excess use of "and" and "the" and sometimes puts a shortened, dialect-enriched form in the mouth of a fictional character.

Dedicated to Bible rereaders everywhere.

Happy (blessed) is the one who reads, and those who hear the words of this prophecy, and keep those things which are written therein: because the time is at hand (Rev 1:3, WZ Paraphrase).

Happy (blessed) is the one who keeps the sayings of the prophecy of this book (Rev 22:7, WZ Paraphrase).

Contents

List of Figures and Tables | xi

Introduction | 1
    Welcome to Adventure! | 1
    What I Mean by "Inductive Reading" | 3
    How to Read Revelation and Daniel Inductively | 4
    Are You Afraid of Interpreting It Wrongly? | 5
    Considering Diversions | 5
    A Disclaimer in Honor of Scholars at Work | 6
    Limits of Inductive Reading | 7
    Helps for Reading Revelation and Daniel | 7
    Original Readers and Others | 8
    What This Book Is Not | 9

1   **Earlier Readers' Stories** | 11
    The Readers in Other Times | 11
    Time of Daniel, 601–538 BCE | 13
    Time of Esther, about 500–480 BCE | 14
    Time of Antiochus IV Epiphanes, 175–164 BCE | 16
    Time of Jesus, 0–30 CE | 17
    Time of John, 20–100 CE | 19
    Time of Constantine, 306–37 CE | 20
    Time of Pope Gregory I, 540–604 | 22
    Time of Islamic Advancement, 632–732 and Eastern Christian Expansion, 685–745 | 24
    Time of Pope Gregory VII, 1015–85 | 26
    Time of Martin Luther, 1483–1546 | 28
    Time of United States Expansion, 1791–1861 | 30
    Time of Global Advancement, 2000–2022 | 33

2　**Lessons from the Sevens** | 42
　　Introduction: Reasons for Seven | 42
　　Seven Churches | 45
　　Seven Seals | 48
　　Seven Trumpets | 51
　　Seven Animals | 54
　　Excursion: Three Angels | 58
　　Seven Plagues | 63
　　Seven Animals Revisited | 65
　　Seven Laments | 72
　　Seven Blessings | 79
　　Conclusion to Lessons from the Sevens | 84

3　**Invitations to Discussion** | 86
　　Introduction: Group Homework and Discussion Guide | 86
　　Rev 1:1–3 | 87
　　Rev 1:4–6 | 87
　　Rev 1:7 | 88
　　Rev 1:8 | 89
　　Rev 1:9–11 | 89
　　Rev 1:12–18 | 90
　　Rev 1:19–20 | 90
　　Rev 2:1–7 | 91
　　Rev 2:8–11 | 91
　　Rev 2:12–17 | 92
　　Rev 2:18–29 | 92
　　Rev 3:1–6 | 93
　　Rev 3:7–13 | 94
　　Rev 3:14–22 | 94
　　Rev 4:1–2 | 95
　　Rev 4:2–8 | 95
　　Rev 4:8–11 | 96
　　Rev 5:1–4 | 96
　　Rev 5:5–7 | 97
　　Rev 5:8–14 | 98
　　Rev 6:1–2 | 98
　　Rev 6:3–4 | 99
　　Rev 6:5–6 | 99
　　Rev 6:7–8 | 100
　　Rev 6:9–11 | 101
　　Rev 6:12–17 | 101
　　Rev 7:1–2 | 102
　　Rev 7:3 | 102
　　Rev 7:4–9 | 103
　　Rev 7:9–14 | 104
　　Rev 7:14–17 | 104
　　Rev 8:1 | 105
　　Rev 8:2–5 | 106
　　Rev 8:6–7 | 106
　　Rev 8:8–9 | 107
　　Rev 8:10–11 | 108
　　Rev 8:12 | 108
　　Rev 8:13—9:11 | 109
　　Rev 9:12–19 | 110
　　Rev 9:20–21 | 110
　　Rev 10:1–4 | 111
　　Rev 10:5–7 | 112
　　Rev 10:8–11 | 112
　　Rev 11:1–2 | 113
　　Rev 11:3–6 | 114
　　Rev 11:7–13 | 114
　　Rev 11:14–15 | 115
　　Rev 11:15–19 | 116

Rev 12:1-2 | 116
Rev 12:3-4 | 117
Rev 12:5-6 | 118
Rev 12:7-9 | 118
Rev 12:10-12 | 119
Rev 12:13-16 | 120
Rev 12:17 | 120
Rev 12:17, Again | 121
Rev 12:17, Third Time | 122
Rev 13:1 | 122
Rev 13:1-8 | 123
Rev 13:9-10 | 124
Rev 13:11-14 | 124
Rev 13:11-18 | 125
Rev 14:1-5 | 126
Rev 14:6-7 | 126
Rev 14:8 | 127
Rev 14:9-11 | 128
Rev 14:12 | 128
Rev 14:13 | 129
Rev 14:14-20 | 130
Rev 15:1-4 | 131
Rev 15:5-8 | 131
Rev 16:1-2 | 132
Rev 16:3-7 | 133
Rev 16:8-11 | 133
Rev 16:12 | 134
Rev 16:13-14 | 135
Rev 16:15 | 135
Rev 16:16 | 136
Rev 16:17-21 | 137
Rev 17:1-7 | 137
Rev 17:7-18 | 138
Rev 18:1-24 | 139
Rev 19:1-6 | 139
Rev 19:6-10 | 140
Rev 19:11-16 | 141

Rev 19:17-21 | 141
Rev 20:1-15 | 142
Rev 20:11-15 | 143
Rev 21:1 | 144
Rev 21:2-4 | 144
Rev 21:5-8 | 145
Rev 21:9-22 | 146
Rev 21:22-27 | 146
Rev 22:1-2 | 147
Rev 22:3-5 | 148
Rev 22:6-10 | 148
Rev 22:11-15 | 149
Rev 22:16-19 | 150
Rev 22:20-21 | 150
Dan 1:1-16 | 151
Dan 1:17-21 | 152
Dan 2 | 152
Dan 2:19-47 | 153
Dan 3 | 154
Dan 3:1-18 | 154
Dan 4 | 155
Dan 5 | 156
Dan 6 | 156
Dan 6:16-25 | 157
Dan 7:1-15 | 158
Dan 7:15-28 | 158
Dan 8:1-14 | 159
Dan 8:1-27 | 160
Dan 9:1-19 | 161
Dan 9:20-27 A | 161
Dan 9:20-27 B | 162
Dan 9:20-27 C | 163
Dan 10 | 163
Dan 11 | 164
Dan 11:32-38 | 165
Dan 12 | 166
Dan 12:1-10 | 167

Appendix 1 | 168
    Verbal Parallels between Daniel and Revelation, page 1 | 169
    Verbal Parallels between Daniel and Revelation, page 2 | 170

Appendix 2 | 172
    Scene and Theme Parallels between Daniel and Revelation, page 1 | 173
    Scene and Theme Parallels between Daniel and Revelation, page 2 | 174
    Scene and Theme Parallels between Daniel and Revelation, page 3 | 175

Appendix 3 | 176
    Sevens in Daniel | 176

Bibliography | 177

Index | 181

List of Figures and Tables

Figure 01: Timeline | 12
Figure 02: Seven Churches | 45
Figure 03: Seven Animals | 56
Figure 04: Seven Animals Revisited | 66
Figure 05: Verbal Parallels between Daniel and Revelation, page 1 | 169
Figure 06: Verbal Parallels between Daniel and Revelation, page 2 | 170
Figure 07: Scene and Theme Parallels between Daniel and Revelation, page 1 | 173
Figure 08: Scene and Theme Parallels between Daniel and Revelation, page 2 | 174
Figure 09: Scene and Theme Parallels between Daniel and Revelation, page 3 | 175
Table 01: Sevens in Daniel | 176

Introduction

WELCOME TO ADVENTURE!

Here you have permission and invitation to read Revelation and its companion book, Daniel, with curiosity and imagination.[1]

Some will say a person cannot read Revelation inductively, that is, simply reading voraciously and watching what pops into the mind and imagination.[2] Some seem to imply that a person must first decide who is the real-life antagonist as represented in the symbols, and then use this presupposition

---

1. For this introduction I researched at least these favorite sources: Brueggemann, *Bible Makes Sense*; Brueggemann, *Prophetic Imagination*; Craddock, *Overhearing the Gospel*; Hayes and Holladay, *Biblical Exegesis*.

2. In Zalabak, "Toward 'Diversity in Cooperation,'" which I wrote in 1996, I gave deductive reasoning for inductive reading. I responded affirmingly to the need for (1) textual, (2) historical, (3) literary, and (4) word analysis in biblical interpretation. I noticed that these steps can be accomplished with deductive logic and received knowledge, and can produce propositions often "written in precise and dogmatic language, ready for the arena of attack" and proof. Then I wrote,

> In my study, I must go farther before application, farther into encounter as well as proposition, into intuitive as well as received knowledge, into inductive as well as deductive logic. These are my further steps:
> (5) Word analysis II: I read and reread, immersing myself in the words of the passage, noticing word frequencies, forms and tenses, synonyms, antonyms, and phonetic families. I let key words and syntax define the passage.
> (6) Literary analysis II: I immerse myself in the passage and those surrounding it, noticing parallels in words, structures, or themes. I create an outline for the book.
> (7) Theological analysis II: I immerse myself in the book and its contextual books within the canon, noticing similarities and differences among authors. I come to a sense of this author's theology.
> (8) Historical analysis II: I immerse myself in the entire canon of Scripture, noticing contemporary, earlier, and later writings and how

as a "method" to determine all the interpretations of the other symbols and scenes before and after the antagonist appears in the writing. Then one can "prove" who the antagonist is. This approach seems to me rather circular. I suppose that, if one tries to be linear (deductive) with something too big for a line, like, say, a sphere, one would have to break in somewhere and, necessarily, the line that results would be circular.

It is true that I have chosen one "method" of three.[3] I have chosen the one that makes the most sense to me given my trust in what the writing claims about its own origins and purposes. For me, the antagonist is not merely a political figure in the past (Preterist Method), nor is the antagonist confined to religion and politics way in the future (Futurist Method). Instead, I see the antagonist much larger, as spreading through all of history, since the prophets wrote and to the end of time (Historicist Method). There is another method described more recently, which intends to remove time factors and only look for present lessons in the prophecies (Idealist Method). All this labeling is more deductive than I hope to be in this book.[4]

Since the third verse in the book of Revelation offers a magnificent promise for those who read this book or hear it read, I propose there must be magnificent benefit in inductive reading. It's like, instead of trying to make a line out of a sphere, I recommend letting the sphere pulse and swarm all around you as you read, while you grasp a little point or a short line or a tiny circle or a miniature sphere here and there out of the big whole.

---

they precipitated or appropriated the words, structure, or theme of the chosen passage.

This section was originally published in *Adventist Today* in the January–February 1996 issue.

3. Here's my simple explanation for the four ways Daniel and Revelation have been interpreted:

Preterism is a school of thought that limits the scope of meaning in Daniel and Revelation to the time from Daniel to Jesus, thinking that the prophecies of afterlife were simply common visions of hope floating in the culture at the time of writing.

Futurism is a school of thought that focuses meaning in Daniel and Revelation on the future, though some reference is understood to Israel and the Jews up until the time of Jesus, or to the church in the first part of Revelation.

Historicism is a school of thought that sees the scope of meaning in Daniel and Revelation as reaching through history from the prophet's time until the end of time, though some reference is understood to cosmic events before the world began.

Idealism is a school of thought that limits the meaning in Daniel and Revelation to ideas, insights, and lessons that can be learned and applied to today's life and world.

4. For easily accessible instances of the historicist method and comparison to the other methods, here are my recommendations: Paulien, *Deep Things of God*; Tucker, *Meeting Jesus*; Stefanovic, *Plain Revelation*; Vetne, *Jesus in the Book of Revelation*.

WHAT I MEAN BY "INDUCTIVE READING"

Let me define early in our time together what I mean by "inductive reading." I do not mean to invite you to place yourself in the biblical picture and imagine and describe what you see from your in-picture perspective. That is a fascinating way to read, and not part of this work. I do not mean to invite you to empty your mind of what you know. Scholars have agreed that we all necessarily look through lenses that limit or shape how and what we see. I do not mean to suggest that I may read and take any piece of Revelation any way it hits me at the moment. I have found amazing connections in biblical contexts and believe that inductive reading will bring those connections together, thus guiding, by the Bible, the interpretation of the Bible.

What I do mean by "inductive reading" is shelving for a moment the list of symbol definitions gleaned from the Bible in previous readings, and letting the definitions burst on your thinking again, maybe in a different order or a different context this time through. What I do mean by "inductive reading" is to leave unopened for now the study guide where you filled in the blanks and to which you return whenever you want to know what you believe, and this time to read straight through Revelation and Daniel. What I do mean by "inductive reading" is to read for the big picture and reread many times to catch new views as seen in a new light from a bigger understanding of the big picture.

What I do mean by "inductive reading" is to put our powers of observation on full alert as we read, noticing anything of what I call "alongside speech." "Alongside speech" brings two ideas into proximity to bring expansion or emotion into the meaning. "Alongside speech" includes repetitions of words or phrases, reappearances of characters or places, and the ways our minds automatically sort the literal thing from the symbol. Other language that I include in "alongside speech" includes figures of speech, metaphor, simile, hyperbole, parable, proverb, riddle, personification, irony, etc. In our day's English most of us can sort these even without extra attention; however, we might need extra pondering on the ancient biblical contexts to observe and sort well what we find in Revelation.

For use in this book, "inductive reading" will mean observing as much as possible in each rereading of Revelation and Daniel and sitting with the information gleaned while the Holy Spirit sorts it in our thinking. That is when, for me, deduction enters as I try to analyze, arrange, and articulate what I learned. I pray God will help me to hold fast what I have, as well as to hold loosely many deductions I might like to see set in stone.

I have discovered that stating my findings with glowing deductive assurance, and with robust logical confidence, can close doors to inquiry for me and for others around me. When I talk as if my conclusion is sure and ordained by God, the very attitude hinders communication. Let me let go for this moment my memorized and well-preserved lists of prophetic symbols and their definitions. Let me read with new eyes what is on the page. Let me invite others with me into this adventure.

HOW TO READ REVELATION AND DANIEL INDUCTIVELY

Here are some habits that help me in reading Revelation and Daniel inductively:

1. Read quickly. Do not stop to interpret; if interpretations flit through your mind, notice and let them flit on by. Do not stop to pronounce correctly. Just read. It should take about an hour. Then read it again.
2. Read as you would a letter from a favorite friend. Even at the mailbox, you tear the letter open, you read quickly, you reach out to grasp the next sentence, you are eager to get to the next paragraph, though you don't really skip any.
3. Read for connection with the mind that wrote it. Read to immerse your mind in the mind of God.
4. Feel free to use audio recordings of the Bible. This way you can "read" while going about your chores, driving on the highways, or going to sleep at night.
5. Read from a variety of translations, perhaps a different version for each day of the week.
6. Set aside an hour each week to read the entire book of Revelation in one sitting. Each of them, Revelation and Daniel, take about an hour to read straight through. If you vary the environment for this reading, you may find surprising connections. Read outdoors. Read with friends. Read aloud in the shower. Read to children. Read on your knees before God.
7. Find someone with whom to share what you learn. This is a most important step. By this means, you open channels through which to receive more. You also connect yourself with the plan of God to save people through simple, personal, individual testimony.

ARE YOU AFRAID OF INTERPRETING IT WRONGLY?

God will give you your blessing for you, yourself, if you read the Bible for yourself. Do you wonder what will keep you from a wrong interpretation? Or did someone else scare you by claiming you'll understand it all wrong? Here are three things to keep in mind.

One. No answer is necessary from you toward detractors. What is necessary is your absolute humility before the sacred word, with no willingness to sit in judgment deciding which pieces of the word of God are useful and which are doubtful, with only a longing recognition that humans don't know everything.

Two. Pray always before reading the Bible. If the Holy Spirit and angels helped in the writing of these words, then it follows surely that the Holy Spirit and angels stand ready to help us understand it.

Three. You don't have to enter into debates, defenses, answers to trick questions, or explanations to detractors, of all that you think about what these things mean to you. When God thinks it is time for you to tell, you will have the words, and God will provide the setting.

CONSIDERING DIVERSIONS

Let us consider a couple diversions that will come to your attention. Some will say that Daniel could not have been written by the Daniel, and at the time, as indicated in the book of Daniel. The first reason cited is that the way it is written requires prophecy, knowing the future before it happens. Since these believe that, of course, no human knows the future before it happens, necessarily then, the book was written after the thing "prophesied." This would imply, of course, that the Bible is not true in its claim about who wrote the book and under what circumstances. I would notice that this idea was first proposed by Porphyry who did it with the intention of tearing down the Christian faith. Instead, I believe that God does equip some humans to foresee the future. In fact, this is one theme asserted in many of Daniel's stories.

Some will say that the book could not have been written by the Daniel who claims in the book to have written it because the stories at the beginning show Daniel as the hero of the story and Daniel would not have written so arrogantly about himself. On the other hand, it's easy to see that the teller of the stories does not make Daniel the hero; he makes God himself the hero. Many times, Daniel is the self-effacing pointer to God as the sovereign Hero.

Some may try to ridicule those who read the stories as if written with Daniel as the author living through the events delineated. More, some may try to ridicule those who trust in the Bible at all, given the many ways they find not to believe what is written regarding how the writing came about. I suggest, don't mind their ridicule; just read.

One more detraction centers around the word "apocalypse." The Greek word simply means "revealing," or "bringing out of secret." The only writing that opens with that word is the book of Revelation, which has literary and linguistic similarities to Daniel. The word "apocalypse" turned out to be such a useful word that people started using it for many other writings which originated during the five hundred years on either side of Jesus's birth, 200 BCE to 300 CE. Since they assign the writing of Daniel into that time period, some three hundred years after the stories claim to have been written, and since it has those obvious similarities to Revelation, Daniel becomes to them only another apocalypse like all the others. Further, one of the most striking characteristics of the other apocalypses is that they were written pseudonymously, often openly taking someone else's name for the author or leaving the author's name blank. The resulting assumption is that both Revelation and Daniel are pseudonymous, also. However, I see no compelling need to group the prototypes of apocalypse with all the others. I see no reason to doubt the real authorship of the Daniel and the John who claim to have written the books.

I remember also this further diversion. There are some who would say that it is neither efficient nor recommended to try to understand Revelation while living in an affluent society. Since it was written in the midst of trauma and societal upheaval, perhaps it cannot be understood if there is no trouble looming. My response is twofold. First, as long as there is anyone marginalized or stigmatized in society, there will be people who can understand. As long as relationship hurts happen there is trauma in society, and Revelation will speak to it. Second, suppose there were no trauma now, the inductive reading of Revelation and Daniel will position their helpful information in our minds ready to be accessible when trauma does hit. There is certainly reason to read Revelation and Daniel now, wherever we are.

A DISCLAIMER IN HONOR OF SCHOLARS AT WORK

Here, I make a disclaimer: I am not disparaging or depreciating the importance of the work that scholars have done in the last two hundred years to examine the dates and contexts of the writing of the sacred books. Without that hard work we might still think all was written only with you and me in mind as the first readers. Instead, we will work at considering what the first readers back then might have understood from the written word, as well as later readers down through history. I encourage us to work hard at considering what readers at critical times in history might have understood, or how they might have re-imagined the text.

Furthermore, neither inductive reading nor I, as such a reader, have any need to discard previous understandings. Inductive reasoning wants as much information as possible, expecting to use that information to formulate something new, while not renouncing the old.

LIMITS OF INDUCTIVE READING

One last caution. Reading inductively like this may not bring us to be able to proclaim with confidence what the church or even our online followers should believe and follow. Raising up a church or a body of followers is an influencer's heavy responsibility, not to be taken lightly. For a church to gain a creed seems to require debate and competition of ideas, creation of leadership hierarchies, and certainly analysis and deduction. In contrast, this material as I work with it is not meant to raise up a following or agreement on minutiae. My work is not intended to build a following for a creed. On the other hand, I would invite many to follow me in reading on their own and often, and again.

Let us read Revelation and Daniel.

HELPS FOR READING REVELATION AND DANIEL

A pen and a journal are my friends and helpers in reading Revelation and Daniel inductively. Here are suggestions for pen and journal reading:

1. Get a notebook you can dedicate to Revelation and Daniel. Make notes about what you discover. Write out your feelings, thoughts, responses, or additional questions. Paraphrase or summarize the Bible passages in your own words.
2. When purchasing Bibles, look for those with easy-to-read print. You may be reading for long periods of time, often, or in various lighting situations. If possible, use at least three very different versions of the Bible, perhaps one from each of the following groups:
    a. KJV (King James Version), NKJV (New King James Version), or MEV (Modern English Version)

b. NRSV (New Revised Standard Version) or NASB (New American Standard Bible)

c. NIV (New International Version), CEV (Contemporary English Version), GNT (Good News Translation), or NLT (New Living Translation)

3. Get a concordance, a Bible dictionary, and a Bible atlas. Make a habit of curiosity about the words and places of the Bible.[5]

4. Always pray before opening the Bible. Pray for the Holy Spirit's guidance, for understanding, and for God's will to be done.

5. Commit to doing these four things repeatedly: Pray, Read, Reflect, Tell.

ORIGINAL READERS AND OTHERS

One support given for placing the antagonist in the past (Preterist Method) is scholars' recognition of the important role of the original readers and hearers of the material. I do believe God performed many miracles over time to preserve the writings and to get them included in our Bible. God could have done this through any number of means, without human help. However, it seems that it was the first readers and then later readers who were used by God for this preservation. We suppose the first readers and later readers would have interpreted the writing in some way helpful to them in their own situation. They apparently found value in Revelation and Daniel. Many scholars cite this or that set of first readers in order to identify something or someone on whom these first readers would have pinned the horrors pictured in the writing. Following these lines, they attempt to theorize the time of the writing to coincide with a past antagonist that would be worthy of the writing. I observe that this past antagonist, though not fulfilling the overarching prophecy, could have been the factor that made Revelation and Daniel favorite reading for God's people at the time and helped them preserve the writings.

This concept of the original readers, and other readers through the centuries, provides infinite realm for research, thought, and imagination. For illustration, let us review how the stories of the deliverance of Israel from Egypt were read and reimagined through the centuries before Daniel was even born.

---

5. For a good set of maps and pictures with background material, I like Wilson, *Revelation*.

The first record of the deliverance of Israel may have been Miriam's song, "Sing to the Lord, for he has triumphed gloriously; the horse and his rider has he thrown into the sea" (Exod 15:21). Then Moses added a lot more words recorded for us in Exod 1:1–19. In many of Moses's later instructions, Moses reminded them that it was the Lord who brought them out Egypt. (You can search online on "brought" and "Egypt" in Exodus, Leviticus, Numbers, and Deuteronomy for amazing retellings of the story.) Joshua repeated the memory, and so did some of the Judges, as did Samuel. Psalms 77–78, 80–81, and 105–6 retell the story; they actually reimagine the story. They tell the story in a way different from its first telling and, in my opinion, likely more applicable to their own time.

In the instance of the deliverance of Israel from Egypt, we have a record of how the holy stories were understood and used in different periods of Israel's history. The creation story is another instance that is told and retold from Gen 1–2. Explore how these tell the story: Exod 20:8–11; Job 38–39; Pss 33; and 104, to name a few.

In light of these examples, let us be brave and do our best to explore by research and imagination how the first readers or hearers, and others later, might have understood the writings of Revelation and Daniel. Let us avoid the method of presupposing with finality who the real-life antagonist would have been to the first readers and those who follow. Instead, let us recognize that they had their tribulations and found spiritual solace in these books by inductive reading. There were enough antagonists and enough tribulations to keep the books of Revelation and Daniel alive.

Please hear my disclaimer about this consideration of original and historical readers. This is not to suggest any "fulfillment" of these prophecies other than that of the grand story overarching all of history. This is not to expect that any one-person antagonist "fulfills" the dark parts of the prophecy. Let us look at history.

WHAT THIS BOOK IS NOT

This book is not academic. It lacks numerous footnotes and a thorough literature review, and its bibliography is not comprehensive.

This book is not totally nonfiction. It has a whole section of fictional stories about people who could have lived at the time specified. These stories are told in order to illustrate the big picture and how inductive reading works.

This book is not liberal or progressive in its understanding of biblical origins. For this author, there will be no dependence on the "documentary hypothesis" or the "synoptic problem." I usually suggest the earliest date available for any biblical writing.

This book is neither futurist, nor preterist, nor proffering a new "fulfillment" or "application" of prophecy. This book falls in the historicist category of prophetic interpretation, with a little extra look at the original setting of the writing, on the one hand, and at some lessons we may draw for today, on the other hand.

This book is not full of definitions and deduction. It is inductive, looking at the big picture. It is one person's summaries and lessons, plus invitations to read for more such summaries and lessons of your own.

This book is not a guide to intuitive reading, as if without conscious reasoning, or as if with some "other" consciousness. It is not a call to "transcend" logic. Instead, this book guides toward inductive reading, which does require reason and logic. This is not a diatribe against deductive logic nor a call to discard past understandings. Inductive reasoning brings everything possible to the reading.

This book is not a biblical commentary in the usual sense of the word. It does not purport to be complete in coverage either of the biblical issues or of the existing literature.

This book presents a happy way to read the book of Revelation, which I call "inductive reading." Three sections approach from three different directions the invitation to read. Fictional stories of readers who must have read inductively show how they were blessed. A step-by-step review of the sets of seven yields some summaries of my current insights and blessings from reading inductively. A set of study and discussion guides invite one into inductive reading by open-ended thought questions and by many biblical cross-references.

This book contains reader-friendly information on the ways people have interpreted Revelation, interpersonal communication tips for tough situations, how to thrive with projects and ventures, what to do when the system runs on fear, shame, and guilt, and continual discovery that God's kingdom is founded on love, acceptance, and forgiveness.

1

Earlier Readers' Stories

THE READERS IN OTHER TIMES

I intend to create some fictional stories of folk in other times who might have read or heard the works of Revelation or Daniel and gained spiritual understanding and consolation from the reading.[1]

My goal is to help people demonstrate for themselves how inductive reading has at least two benefits toward the deductive goal that seems blessed and popular. Inductive reading calls for reading many times, over and over again, as distinguished from a deductive reading by which the reader decodes the symbols and times and then reads by code and certainty. I propose that the many times reading will, number one, help the reader to clarify the deduction for him or herself, and it will, number two, help the mind to retain and explain the processes of that deduction.

This is not a presentation to introduce or even support "multiple fulfillments" of these prophecies. This is not to detract from, or give "alternative interpretations" for, the one grand, overarching fulfillment for which I believe God gave these prophecies.

---

1. My research for these stories included these resources: Bowman, *Christianity*; Curtis et al., *100 Most Important Events in Christian History*; Doukhan, *Secrets of Daniel*; Doukhan, *Secrets of Revelation*; Emmerson and McGinn, *Apocalypse in the Middle Ages*; Koester, *Revelation and the End*; Kung, *Catholic Church*; Lynch, *Medieval Church*; Maxwell-Stuart, *Chronicle of the Popes*; Tomkins, *Short History of Christianity*; Wainwright, *Mysterious Apocalypse*; Walker, *History of the Christian Church*; Wengst, *Pax Romana*; White, *Great Controversy*.

These stories will illustrate how people could have been persuaded to keep the books of Revelation and Daniel in our Bibles because of the spiritual blessings they received from reading them while waiting along the journey of the grand fulfillment. They may show us how we can hold ourselves attentive to Revelation though the journey be long.

Here is a caution about these stories: I remind us that we cannot enter fully the thought patterns, the fears and joys, or the reactions of historical people. I am continually hounded and bounded by the lenses of my time. Admitting this limitation, I think there is benefit in researching and exploring, as best we can, what might have been a possible reaction to Revelation and Daniel in specific previous times.

We need a timeline by which to tell these stories. For this overarching timeline, I will mark general times by the hundred years. Then I will fill in specific stories with more specific dates. You will want to refer back to this page.

Timeline

Name	Date
Adam	1000
Noah	600
Abraham	500
Moses	300
David	0
Daniel, Babylon	100
Esther, Persia	300
Antiochus IV Epiphanes, Greece	500
Jesus, Rome	700
John	1000
Constantine	1500
Pope Gregory I	1800
Islamic Advancement	2000
Pope Gregory VII	
Martin Luther	
United States Expansion	
Global Advancement	

Admittedly, this timeline falls far short of inclusivity. Here we lack stories from the Far East and Africa except for Egypt. There is nothing from the Americas until 1800. At this point in my studies, I would not be able to speak knowledgeably of stories from those places. What we have here will be sufficient, I think, to get us into reading Revelation and Daniel.

TIME OF DANIEL, 601-538 BCE

"Bennie, did you hear the latest story from the palace?" queried Ruth, running to the field with the lunch Mother had prepared for Bennie and his dad who were working in the wheat.

"What now?" He was happy to stop work, though his sister could talk too much.

"This is the best yet," she answered. "This Daniel survived a night in the lions' den! The king put him there because some people lied, yet he didn't get hurt even a bit!"

Barry had come to help for a while; he was Babylonian and had recently lost rights as the favored class.

"More stories about this Daniel?" Barry groused. "And I suppose you really do think you will all go back to Jerusalem soon, too."

"Oh, yes!" said Ruth. "Daniel has been having visions and dreams about it. Really, we were sent here for only seventy years, and that time is nearly finished."

Dad sat on a nearby rock, looking off into the far distance as he often did. Then he said something he often said, "If only the Messiah would come soon!"

"Barry, you remember our stories from the past," continued Ruth. "How the world and universe was created by a God who is most lovingly and generously good. And how Adam, the first human, turned away from that God and there's been an enemy in the world ever since."

"Yes," said Barry. "I wish I could really believe in a God like that."

"You can," said Bennie, reviving now that he had food in his stomach. "Noah believed in a God like that, and God used Noah to save all believers from a huge flood, just like he's saved Daniel and some others from big troubles, according to the stories that come from the palace."

"Then Abraham was called by God to father our great nation," said Dad. "He knew the Messiah would come one day to free the world of this great intruder enemy and restore our face-to-face ability with this wonderful God. Abraham waited a long time for the son God had promised, and sure enough the son was born."

"Then we all had to go to Egypt," Ruth chimed in. "And they made us slaves there, but Moses under God brought all of Israel out of Egypt with no fighting and much loot. We thought surely God would pull us back to himself in a land he gave us for our own."

"Then why are you here? Way over in Babylon?" asked Barry.

Bennie answered, "David was a great king almost five hundred years ago, now. We thought one of his sons would be the Messiah. Then the other kings after him turned their backs on God, and nearly seventy years ago, Babylon's armies ruined our city and took us captive."

"Yah, I guess I knew that," said Barry. "You don't belong here. And now I don't belong here, with Persia taking over. What is this Messiah you keep talking about?"

Dad helped out on this answer. "They say Daniel has been having dreams. You probably heard about that one dream it was said Daniel interpreted for the king a few years ago. Daniel said it showed new kingdoms coming in the future, and especially the kingdom of God. Now Daniel's dreams sort of follow the same pattern, with parts of them quite scary. Then right in the middle of those dreams is a piece of the most fabulous light. My friends think it means the Messiah will come soon to restore everything we have lost. He will rebuild our temple and vindicate our worship. Oh, the words reported as spoken in those dreams speak joy in my soul because they remind me of the old ways in Jerusalem."

"Dad, do you think we will see the Messiah?" asked Ruth.

"I don't know. We must wait patiently, my child. Do hang onto hope. Hope is always good."

TIME OF ESTHER, ABOUT 500–480 BCE

"I've been on my feet all day," groaned Beth as she came into the dressing room. She saw immediately that her best friend Dina was not yet in from her work in the Queen's quarters. She lay on her bed and thought. There was so much to think about. There was Abel to think about. Dark curly hair. Sparkling eyes. And the things he could tell her about the scrolls! What a guy.

"Beth, of all things, what are you doing lying on the bed with your servant clothes on?" Dina entered. "You'll get them all wrinkled and unacceptable."

"I was just thinking," said Beth. "You know Abel has been reading Daniel."

"Oh, Abel again. Who's Daniel?"

"Apparently, he was a famous courtier, old by the time Persia took over. He survived miracles. He had dreams. Abel thinks that scroll should for sure be kept with the holy writings."

"So, tell me about some of these miracles and dreams."

"Daniel was a Jew brought from Israel by Nebuchadnezzar," said Beth. "He passed all the training and tests with top marks and got the place next to the king. He interpreted a dream for the king that showed our Persia stepping in after Babylon, and some other kingdoms after Persia, and ending with God's kingdom. Abel says it's fascinating reading."

"Well, I'm hungry," said Dina. "Let's go to the food hall, and you can tell me more." On their way, Dina blurted, "Oh I forgot to tell you, the Queen has ordered all her servants to fast and pray. It seems there's some great disaster looming. She hasn't been herself for days now."

They went on to the food hall. Fasting could start tomorrow. They were happy to see some of their friends there, but shocked to see the King's best man in the food hall.

"Hey Beth," said Dina, "what do you make of that Haman? He doesn't usually come here, does he?"

"Hmmmm, I wonder what's up," responded Beth. "He really does give me the creeps. I had to get out of his way today in one of the back hallways, and of course I had to curtsey and bow. He gets really angry if you miss something like that."

"Well, I don't know, but I saw a decree today with his signature. It's a signed law that all Jews are to be killed," said Dina.

"No! Who could be so mean as all that?" exclaimed Beth.

"I think Haman could," said Dina. "Tell me more about your Abel."

"Yes! Abel thinks part of that Daniel scroll talks about a Messiah coming to save all the Jews, but there's a lot of mean and violent stuff that happens before we get to that place in the scroll."

"Dina," said Beth, "what do you think about the Jews' God? I hear this is supposed to be a thoroughly good God, loving and generous. Abel thinks he is better than all our other gods. Abel's been reading other scrolls, too, stories about how this God delivered his people in ages long gone."

"I'm not too sure," said Dina. "If I didn't know this Queen Esther, I think I would continue to believe, as I did before, that there is no God or person, with power, that can be generous and good. I think she is that way."

"What if Haman is that bad antagonist that Abel has read about in the scrolls?" said Beth. "What if Haman will kill the Jews and then the Queen and whoever else? Does the Queen seem frightened?"

"Not really. That's the strange part. She trusts this God of the Jews and she's not scared, but she did order us to fast and pray," said Dina.

"I think I like those other stories of surviving miracles," said Beth. "I think I'll ask Abel to tell me some of those. What if we could survive a miracle?"

TIME OF ANTIOCHUS IV EPIPHANES, 175-164 BCE

"Whoa there, Onan," called Simon from his meditation corner as Onan bounded into the room with energy. "Onan, tell me again, when were our Scriptures translated into this Greek language?"

"That was about a hundred years ago," answered Onan. "Are you reading Daniel again?"

"Yes, I can't help it. There is so much to ponder when I read Daniel."

"Well, it might do you more good to ponder some of our later philosophers, Simon."

"Yes, I know. I agree with updating our systems. The gymnasium is a good idea so we can get along better with our neighbors and have people of other nations come here to train and maybe to worship with us." Simon paused then continued.

"But the book of Daniel seems so prescient of our time, as if it was written right now by the scribe next door. So, help me out with the history, Onan. You are so much better with the dates than I am."

"Babylon captured Israel in several forays around 430 years ago. Then Persia got control about 370 years ago. Alexander the Greek came racing through about 170 years ago. Yes, these kingdoms did rule in order just like Daniel said they would," said Onan in quick review of the events both he and Simon knew because of Daniel.

"We've been the crossroads of wars for 150 years," sighed Simon. "How I wish Messiah would come!"

"There you are, groaning again!" said Lucas who had walked in just in time to hear Simon's longing. Lucas was naked and dripping with perspiration. "What you need is some real games. Not only do I win physical feats, but now also I'm starting to win at military strategies. This is where Israel's future lies!" said Lucas as he toweled himself, letting his muscles swell and ripple for the effect on the two other young men.

Simon looked up from the scroll. "Lucas, listen to this. The Daniel scroll says that 'the people of the prince will destroy the city and the temple, then they will be cut off with a flood and destroyed. The prince will make a covenant with the people for one week and in the midst of that week the sacrifices will be stopped. And he will put an abomination at the altar, and this will cause the desolation of the people' (Dan 9:26-27 KJV, WZ paraphrase). Don't you see, Lucas and Onan, this is the week."

"You mean you really think our Greek Antiochus IV is the antagonist in Daniel?" exclaimed Onan. "You think this is the pivotal week of all history?"

"You can't really go there, Simon," said Lucas. "This week has been proclaimed for some celebration. They left our Sabbath alone. They made the primary celebration mid-week so we wouldn't have to worry."

"Don't you know, Lucas, that the sacrifices have been stopped, made illegal now since that mid-week event. This Antiochus calls himself God. And I hear that some have seen the feast dish of a whole roasted pig set there by the altar in our temple. It's a drastic disrespect, I tell you. It is the seeds of our desolation!"

"What do the scrolls say about how this prince will die?" asked Onan.

"Well, I don't know what it means that a flood will come since Jerusalem is in the hills," said Simon. "Maybe it refers back to the deliverance from Egypt, that our deliverance will be that complete. There is another place in Daniel where the writing says, 'he will come to his end and there will be no one to help him'" (Dan 11:45 KJV, WZ paraphrase).

Lucas was unimpressed. "Wars continue always. I will go to war. It is the only going excitement and always will be."

Onan expressed his concern and then his strategy: "There's really not much we can do about all this, Daniel or no Daniel. But wait, doesn't Daniel say something about the Messiah? I will await the Messiah."

Simon answered, "I will read the scrolls. I will read Daniel."

TIME OF JESUS, 0–30 CE

"I'm going to study well at school so I can read the scrolls," said Joseph who was son to Nicodemus. The one with bright eyes looking into his was Rebekah, newly discovered daughter to Photina and young trusted maid in Pilate's household. In fact, Pilate's wife had taken a special liking to Rebekah.

"Oh, I too long to read the scrolls," said Rebekah. "I have heard that when kings from the east came looking for a new Jewish king, all the scribes read the scrolls to find where the Messiah would be born."

"Yes," said Joseph, "and the writings of Daniel give dates and time spans for when the Messiah would come. The time is now. The time is right. Rebekah, we might get to see the Messiah! Wouldn't that be most fabulous!"

"I wish I could be the mother of the Messiah," whispered Rebekah, knowing it was the whisper of every girl's heart in Israel. But then, she wasn't really one of those girls anymore. She'd been raised in a God-fearing home, reciting prayers and scriptures like everyone else. Then two weeks ago, she had met her real mom, a Samaritan, and now she didn't belong anywhere. Mom Photina said her father was a Jewish man, so now she knew she was of mixed blood. Rebekah wondered, "Will I ever fit in again?"

Joseph reached out to her tenderly. "We'll figure it out," he said kindly.

Joseph's father, Nicodemus, passed by them as they sat on the bench by the road. He hardly looked at them, and then he brightened, turned back, and said, "This Jesus I've been telling you about, he said we should read and understand Daniel. Somehow, I've known it was an important scroll. Now I'm going after it."

"Oh, let us read together, all three of us, please. I want to understand it, too." That was Rebekah's heart cry, and then she realized it would be Joseph's privilege and not her own to learn to read the scroll. She dropped her eyes to study the dust of the road.

After a moment to think, Nicodemus invited them both to his study at mid-afternoon today. What excitement! Until then, Joseph would go to school, and Rebekah would go to the palace to serve Pilate's wife.

"Are you happy about something then, my star Rebekah?" asked the beautiful woman.

"Oh, yes, my lady. I will begin today reading with a scholar the scroll of Daniel. This is the source of my joy."

"Daniel, the Jewish scroll?"

"Yes, my lady. Joseph says there are prophecies in that scroll that have already come true, like knowing that Persia would follow Babylon and Greece would follow Persia and Rome would follow Greece." Rebekah gushed on, "I want to learn what Daniel wrote about the Messiah."

"Alright, yes. Be sure and tell me what you learn, my dear. Now we have work to do."

On her way to study, Rebekah thought about what Photina had told her the day she found her. Photina had left Rebekah as a baby on the doorstep of a Jewish family, hoping they would take her in. Photina loved her baby yet had no way to bring up a child in her battered lifestyle and with so few resources. Then Photina had met this man named Jesus and he restored everything to her. She said she lived a better life because of meeting Jesus and had spent more than a year searching for her lost child. Now this same Jesus was urging them to read and understand Daniel.

They read that night about the Messiah coming and being cut off and having nothing. It seemed a big puzzle to Rebekah. Nicodemus seemed sure that this seventy-week prophecy was how they know it's time for the Messiah to show up.

"There's more that's puzzling about Jesus's comments last evening," said Nicodemus. "He warned about seeing this sin that seeds for desolation standing in the holy place as Daniel wrote. That's when we have to leave immediately, Jesus said."

"I don't know what that means," said Joseph, "but I surely do know I want to continue reading Daniel!"

TIME OF JOHN, 20-100 CE

"Lois, come, the letter will be read at the house of Antipas today!" exclaimed Sylvia.

"The letter?" asked Lois.

"John's letter from prison," answered Sylvia. "They say it's just as fascinating as Daniel's dreams."

"I don't feel much like going over there," said Lois. "I don't see how they can open their house for meetings so soon after Antipas's death. It won't ever be the same again in that house."

"Yes, Babylon won that round against Jesus," agreed Sylvia, using the common Christian code name for the Roman Empire, Babylon, like the empire in Daniel's day. "Certainly Antipas was a martyr for Jesus."

They found the house of Antipas warm and inviting and filling up with their neighbors. The son of Antipas was set to read, and first made an introductory speech. "They call this the Golden Age of Rome," he said, "but we know it is the Iron Kingdom foretold by Daniel. They want us to call their emperor the son of god, but we know Jesus is the son of God. They have built roads and schools and exercise fields, banks and baths and libraries, aqueducts and postal services, but we know they took poor people's land and living to do it. They proclaim the power of peace, but we know that peace kept by power is poisoned peace."

The son of Antipas continued, "We will read today a most important document, written by our beloved pastor, John, while in prison. Let us pay close attention now." And he read to the Church in Pergamum, the book of Revelation.

Sylvia and Lois stayed a bit longer to visit with their neighbors, and much of their conversation reviewed the reading they had heard.

Someone said, "Do you suppose John was wondering about the future when Jesus came to him on Patmos, just like the king of Babylon in Daniel's day was pondering the future when he got that dream?"

"That's interesting," said Sylvia. "There were some sentences in that document that point the hearer to the future, what will be hereafter."

Someone else commented, "Surely the Golden Age of Rome won't like this document, showing the real Son of God, and using our code name for Rome. It's a thin cover, and surely the Empire will know."

"I thought about that, too," said Lois. "It's got to be read to all the seven churches John frequented and more, so we'd better take extremely good care to protect that document."

Another comment mentioned the animals. "Did you notice that the animals in this document are of the same species and similar descriptions as those in Daniel? I wonder who the antagonist is in this layout of things."

"Oh, Rome, of course!" blurted another.

Sylvia muttered to Lois, "Seems to me it's a much bigger antagonist than the mere Roman Empire."

"And you'd better watch your words, friend," said Lois, "Roman ears and spies don't want to hear about anything being bigger than Rome."

"Indeed," granted Sylvia, and they listened some more.

One of the teenagers said, "I have a great yearning to hear that document read again and again. I may hike over to Thyatira to hear it there. There's something in it that speaks to me in my heart, as if Jesus himself were here talking to me." Several nodded or otherwise agreed.

Then Sylvia got a far-off gleam in her eye and had some excitement in her voice when she said, "Look here, Lois. The coming of the Messiah was prophesied in Daniel, and the stories of Daniel prepared the people for the coming. I think, if the second coming of the Messiah is prophesied in this Revelation, that hearing the document read will prepare us for this coming."

They chose a strong man to go with the messenger carrying the document, so it could be preserved for all the churches until Jesus should come.

TIME OF CONSTANTINE, 306-37 CE

"Cato, what was that all about? We've forded a lot of rivers in our time as legionnaires, but I've never seen such drama and words to attend the strategy. And wealth. Did you see the bishop's rings and staff and other jewelry? Looks like he might be as wealthy as our Emperor Constantine."

"Didn't you remember, Aurelius? Today is the day of our baptism! Now we are Christians."

"What did you say we are?" asked the incredulous Aurelius.

"Christians. The Emperor Constantine wants to solidify his empire. If we're all Christians, we will all celebrate the same holidays and worship on the same days. Then those can be marketed as if there were no others."

"I think I do remember some mention of this baptism," said Aurelius. "I heard the emperor Constantine is making no plans for his own baptism, however."

"Yes, that hesitation of his has me puzzled," said Cato. "He insists that we ride through the roaring river to be baptized, and he won't do it himself. Such a short-sighted Emperor!"

"Oh, I think maybe he has some long vision." countered Aurelius. "I heard he plans to move the capital of the Roman Empire over to Byzantium and call it Constantinople. There he can start over in the new religion, without all the Roman god stories and statues that permeate the land and city of Rome."

"And he can force everybody to be baptized on the way to leaving behind the old ways," said Cato. "I wonder who will take over the power in the city when the empire moves its seat to Constantinople."

"The bishop, of course," observed Aurelius, and they both instantly knew the bishop could do that.

"Titus!" they both said his name together, and Cato followed up. "Let's see what Titus thinks about today's work. You know he was raised a Jew and then became Christian because he wanted to. I hear him coming now."

"Yes, let's ask him," agreed Aurelius. "I hear the Christians have some nearly sacred writings of very interesting prophecies."

"Titus, we're all Christians now!" they beamed at their roommate, another of the best, a legionnaire."

"What?" chuckled Titus. "What do you mean?"

"By emperor's orders we rode through a deep and high rapids today to be baptized. The bishop was there with much show of wealth and many strange words. We've been baptized like you."

Titus, in great astonishment, asked, "Do you even know what a Christian is and does?"

"You teach us," said Cato.

Shaking his head to himself he said, "Well, there's one of our writings that you simply must read. It was written after Jesus was here and died and rose and went away. It is a story of what happened when Jesus came back to visit with John. It's called Apocalypse, the Revelation of Jesus Christ."

"Is that the one that talks about a great antagonist who will arise?" asked Aurelius.

"Sure," said Titus. "We've started calling him the antichrist, anti-christ, you get it?"

"So, who is he?" pushed Cato.

"Well, we think there will be one specific mega-antichrist at the end of time, and we also think there are many antichrists, from now to the end of time, who will show the spirit of antichrist in troubling God's people. It's like we believe Jesus is already here now, but not yet here in the fullness of his kingdom. So the antichrist is already among us now, but not yet fully manifested."

"I can think of only two candidates for that title at this time," said Aurelius. "There's the emperor, who forces conversions yet won't himself take the name of Christian. And then there's that Christian bishop who seems set up to take the power of force in this city once the emperor moves the capitol."

"How can we get a copy of this apocalypse writing?" asked Cato. "I want to read it for myself."

TIME OF POPE GREGORY I, 540-604[2]

"After the death of her husband, that Silvia has become more and more reclusive," commented Isabella.

"Oh, I think she's just closer and closer to Christ and wants to spend her time with him," countered Margarita.

"Yes, reclusive," said Isabella. "You know her son, before he became Pope, built several monasteries on family land both here in Rome and on Sicily. I suppose she will take the vows to commit her life to serve Christ soon."

"You know," added Margarita, "Gregory didn't want to be pope, and he has kept his monk's ways, never strutting with the power as the other bishops did. He was pressed into service when the bishop before him died of the plague."

"And look at all he has done," Isabella picked up the thread again. "We had such tragic breakdown of all Roman infrastructure and conveniences, and then we had war for so many years, that it's even hard to remember the aqueducts that brought us water and the baths, the temples and the money, the books and the roads. Have you noticed how not many of the younger generation can even read now? Crime has become commonplace, and the plague has ravaged the land.

"Pope Gregory has ministered faithfully in the midst of all the trouble. He often gives to the poor. He stops the invasions and converts the invaders. He sends missionaries to far countries. He continues to call himself the 'servant of the servants of God.'"

When Isabella paused for breath, Margarita added some accounts of her own. "They say he's collecting a library, and Victoria tells me he's writing more books, always writing. He's writing about how to get along with each

---

2. My research for this story included Sivaramamurti and Straw, "St. Gregory the Great."

other, how the church should be run, about the Bible, and about things he has seen. Victoria thinks he will be known in the future as great."

"He certainly preaches well, writes nice liturgy, and cares about the music, too," said Isabella. Then she added, "I wonder when Victoria will come have lunch with us again. She is always so interesting with stories about life in Pope Gregory's household."

"Victoria!" exclaimed Margarita. "I almost forgot. She's coming over tonight for supper with us."

"Very well," said Isabella. "Let's keep the meal simple, and bring up from the cellar some of that most delightful wine from Sicily."

Indeed, Victoria was full of stories of her days in the shadow of the Pope. She said he was so pious you felt like God was in the house. "He thinks all of us should live in piety," she said, "and then he wants someone to go to market and negotiate food prices among the hagglers there. It's almost impossible to keep your God-focus there."

"Oh, and talk about piety," said Victoria, "Today Pope Gregory called the Bishop of Constantinople 'Antichrist'! Well, at least he said that bishop was showing pride, which is the spirit of Antichrist, in his desire to be called the 'ecumenical' or 'universal' patriarch."

"I've heard that Pope Gregory has a burning sense that he is living in the last days," commented Margarita.

"Yes," said Victoria. "I saw some of his notes the other day. I don't know if they were for something he was writing or just something he had read. There was the name Victorinus with the date 300, and then Jerome with the date 400, and then Primasius with the date 551. Victorinus's commentary on the Apocalypse seems to be the earliest one we have. Then Jerome and Primasius continued and elaborated on his work. Victorinus proposed the theory of recapitulation, that the sevens recapitulate each other. Primasius outlined the first of his commentary according to the first three sets of seven. That really makes a lot of sense to me. There seems to be a marvelous rhythm in the text."

That was longer and deeper than Victoria usually talked, yet the other two women sat spellbound. This was talk they longed to hear. They would read the Apocalypse again before retiring, trying to sense its natural divisions, and how those natural progressions and cadences worked.

TIME OF ISLAMIC ADVANCEMENT, 632–732 AND EASTERN CHRISTIAN EXPANSION, 685–745[3]

"I think the merchandise is all here, Friend Sergius," said Balthus, one Christian merchant to another. "God has protected us along the way. Let us finish our business, and then I have much news to tell you and those who will come at your call."

"You are our benefactor, Blessed Balthus. We thrive on your fabrics, your spices, your gems, and your dyes, and our need is deep and strong for your news, your greetings from far away fellow Christians, and your reports of how they read the scrolls."

Sergius paid Balthus in weighed gold, and they sat down at a rough-hewn table with a little wine, bread, and cheese to wait for the others to come. When the room was full, Balthus began.

"Dear Brothers and Sisters in Christ," he said. "I bring grace and peace from God and greetings with love from Christians who are thriving all the way from Rome to India, and even from those farther north. The trade routes are pleasant, and Christians welcome us everywhere.

"Let me recall your minds to the fact that eight out of the last ten popes here in Rome came from beyond Constantinople in the east. In the same way as Pope Gregory sent missionaries to England and Germany, the churches in the east have sent missionaries to India and China, while the Patriarch in Constantinople has sent missionaries to Russia. Praises be to God!

"You also recall than since Muhammad died in 632, more than 100 years ago now, Islam has advanced with great rapidity, overtaking the Persian empire and subjugating the peoples south of Constantinople and around the south of the Mediterranean Sea all the way to Spain. They were stopped twice at Constantinople, and didn't make it past Spain to reach Rome, but the other cities of Christian leadership are no longer active with bishops and buildings. Antioch, Jerusalem, and Alexandria are in the hands of Islam.

"Generally, when the armies come through and pass on, Christians in the east are left undisturbed to worship as they wish. You remember that the Christians there are of two different persuasions regarding how the nature of Christ did or did not blend the divine and human natures. These Nestorians and Jacobites get along alright in the same lands."

Sergius stood, brought some more bread, and then spoke to Balthus in front of the congregated believers.

---

3. My research for this story included Jenkins, *Lost History of Christianity*.

"We send our greetings to all Christians on your route, be they Western Romans, Eastern Romans, Nestorians, or Jacobites. We pray for the Lord's protection to go with you and watch over the churches of our Christ wherever they are."

A hearty "Amen" filled the room, yet they all still sat silent, chewing on some bread or cheese or sipping some wine or water. No one really wanted to leave. Then someone called from the back of the room. "Tell us, What do they say about the scrolls? How do other Christians understand the Apocalypse?" Heads nodded.

Balthus began again. "My dear fellow Christians, I have worshiped in many churches and attended many study meetings like this, and I listen carefully. I will tell you what I hear.

"In the Western Roman empire, the people have inherited the biblical methods that were taught in Alexandria, giving them a ready interpretive method for all the Bible. Accordingly, I hear more and more often the Apocalypse mentioned in the same breath as the Song of Solomon. As the Song is interpreted as an allegory, or parable, of Christ and the church, so the Apocalypse is interpreted as an allegory, or parable, of the church in the Christian age. Allegory is a ready, at-hand method because the reader can pick any piece of the writing and creatively apply its pictures and ideas to the present experience.

"In the East the people inherited the methods used by a cadre of colleagues in Antioch. They have a method fully dependent on the words of the Bible, reading carefully the words and the immediate context, noticing those in a wider context of the book of the Bible and then of the whole Bible, and of the historical milieu out of which it came. So in the east, the context must be respected, and the Apocalypse must be read over and over again, listening to rhythms, repetitions, and similarities within it and connecting it with the whole Bible. The Christians talk together and share what they see and hear. I think they take the story of John on Patmos as real experience and the account of what he saw and heard as real experience. I think they allow that the repeated sevens may recapitulate each other. And with the main eastern Christian church located in the eastern capital in Seleucia-Cresiphon, the site of old Babylon, they probably read the Apocalypse alongside of the Daniel scroll. There are traditions there that still remember Daniel and revere his writing."

Again, the people sat quietly with murmured amens and head nods. Then that same person in the back of the room said, "Sergius, will you let us come here for the next three nights? Will you read to us the Apocalypse? You can get the scroll, surely. Then will you read Daniel, too?"

And all the others looked expectantly at Sergius, with a bit more light in their eyes than they had when they came in.

TIME OF POPE GREGORY VII, 1015-85

Louis looked at his small scrap of parchment. He had drawn columns with seven rows in each column. This was not his first try at this. He sat at a table in the quiet space of the cathedral library. He knew it was a small library as libraries go, but his fellow students and the master were grateful for the number of volumes they had. Besides that, the master had gone to great expense and effort to have brought from England, at Louis's own request, a copy of the three volumes of the Venerable Bede's (ca. 673-735) commentary on the Apocalypse. Though the commentary was now more than three hundred years old, its ideas fed Louis's mind exactly what he craved.

Louis had already studied the *City of God* (413-26) and Augustine's insistence that there is no future millennium of bliss, but that the church is currently in its millennium. He had read every Apocalypse commentary he could find since Augustine and found himself impatient with the numerous, commonplace, allegorical interpretations that seemed capable of readings wildly inconsistent among authors as well as unfitting and disrespectful to the contexts in the Apocalypse itself. He longed for clues to readings that would completely honor the words of the text.

Louis thought he had found it in Bede's commentaries. Because of Bede, Louis had also studied the commentaries of Primasius (527-65), who wrote more than two hundred years before Bede and influenced Bede's ideas.

This is what Louis had on his drawing. First, he had made seven rows down for the seven churches of the Apocalypse. Then he made rows across for the parts of the letters: descriptions of the author, what Jesus's knows, what Jesus advises, and promises to the overcomer. He entered carefully the words of the text that fit in each resultant cell of the graph. He looked for repetitions, similarities, and differences. He understood why Bede had said this was a picture of the church down through time, and that idea only made him want to tie the outline to dates in history. However, Bede had left the dates undefined.

Louis searched for another scrap of parchment and on it he made a another, similar graph, this time with the seven churches listed down the side. Then he put the seven seals in the next column, and the seven trumpets in the next column. He added a column for the seven last plagues. He always put in the exact words of the text, though he sometimes caught himself automatically inserting something he had picked up from the allegories. Louis was a exacting scholar.

For yet another day, Louis closed the big scrolls and put them carefully on the shelf. He found such joy and purpose in reading the Apocalypse, he would come here again when he got a chance.

"Andre, how are you?" Louis greeted his friend who had taken this day off from studies to ride out into the country and visit his friends in a monastery not far out.

"I'm tired," said Andre, "and happy. Those monks surely do pray a lot and we didn't get to visit much, but I do respect their prayers."

"Oh," said Andre, "I heard some real news at a pub where I stopped on the way back. Seems as though Emperor Henry IV gave in because of the Pope Gregory VII's excommunication and went over the Alps to make penance. And now Gregory has finally agreed to absolve Henry as long as Henry stays out of the Pope's business of choosing and installing church personnel."

"Well, that fits," said Louis. "I think Pope Gregory VII has been interested for some time in cleaning up the church appointment processes, especially to purge the opportunities to purchase church positions. Further, since his *Dictatus Papae* (1075) a couple years ago, it's quite clear who expects to rule the world, at least in all of Europe. That dictation says that the Pope is 'universal,' unique, and judged by no one, and that the Roman Church never did and never will err, and is the only catholic church."

"And it's not so very long ago," Andre continued, "while this Pope, then called Hildebrand, was already powerful in the church, that the Pope in Rome (Leo IX) and the Patriarch in Constantinople excommunicated each other (1054). That schism stuck and the west is going its own way now without the east. Hildebrand became Gregory VII, and now rules uninhibited."

"Andre," said Louis. "I'm not as interested in the fares of popes and emperors as perhaps I should be. I have found something that holds my attention on Christ more surely than anything I've ever read before."

"Apocalypse again?" queried Andre.

"Yes, it feeds my hunger, it walks as my companion, it makes each day worthwhile. I wish you would look at the drawings I made today, and together perhaps we can make sense of them."

"Didn't the master mention a book from last century, a handbook of the Antichrist?" remembered Andre. "Will he try to get a copy of that for us, too?"

"Oh, I'm not so interested in Antichrist traditions as I am in the very words of the text of this writing," said Louis. "However, I do hope the master will get a copy of that handbook. I heard that it takes seriously the words of

Daniel, discussed by Jerome, and of 2 Thessalonians, addressed by Haimo, and of the Apocalypse, considered by Bede. I'm sure it would interest me."

Later, after some moments of silence, Louis asked, "Will you have time to look at my work this evening? Tomorrow we go back to school, and there is so much I want to think about."

TIME OF MARTIN LUTHER, 1483–1546[4]

"Sometimes I wish I'd gone with Marie Katharina. You know I could have." So moped Marie Helena after a frustrating day in the cloister. Restlessness was in the air. All patience was fraying.

"I heard they all got husbands except Katharina herself," put in Marie Veronica.

"Oh, she's probably got her eye on someone," said Helena, "and she'll get him, too."

"Helena, do you remember how she used to talk such interesting ideas about the Apocalypse? We could continue her research. It seemed to energize her. Maybe it would lighten our lives," suggested Veronica.

"She used to spend hours over in the library, said she was reading the Bible kept safe there. The Apocalypse, she said. And after long hours she would come away with a light in her eyes," observed Helena. "Could we ask the Mother Superior for a chance to look at the writings of that man Joachim of Fiore (1130 or 1135 to 1201 or 1202)?" Helena was coming to life over the ideas.

This is how it happened that Helena and Veronica began spending as much time in the library as they could, around their other duties. They discovered there were several monks who had studied and written about the Apocalypse after Joachim yet some two hundred years before their time.

"Apparently people back then wanted to find meaning in history," said Veronica. "These all reject the allegorical readings and show periods of history, some more minutely delineated than others."

"It's a lot to comprehend. I have a hard time remembering this and that and another detail," said Helena.

"Let's make a chart!" said Veronica. "You know that new substance called paper? I think the Mother has some; I saw a piece the other day. I'll see if she will give us a page, and some ink, too. We can write it all down and see it better."

"What if we write wrong?" said Helena.

---

4. My research for this story included Edwards, "Apocalypticism Explained: Martin Luther."

"We'll just have to be careful," said Veronica.

So Helena and Veronica made charts. They were very careful to use only the words of the sacred writings in their charts.

Veronica kept a running descriptive conversation. "First column, letters to seven churches, which some people think refer to the on-marching periods of church history. Second column, opening the seven seals, which some people think is a picture of how the church fared through history."

Helena noticed the parallels. "So wouldn't that make these two columns somewhat similar down the stages, both referring to church history?"

"Indeed it would," answered Veronica. "Third column, sounding the seven trumpets, which is more difficult to match with either history or the first two columns. Fourth column, shall we call this the two animals or shall we skip over these animals for lack of seven distinct divisions?"

"Let's include it," said Helena. "We may find something."

"Fifth column," continued Veronica, "dumping the seven vials, which. . . . Oh, look, Helena, see how words are repeated and similar in the trumpets and the vials!"

"Yes, I thought we'd find something like that. And I also think we'll find amazing parallels and repetitions if we'll go bring in Daniel about those two animals. I seem to remember some very interesting similar word pictures in Daniel." Helena was the artistic one.

"We've got to put this away and go for evening prayers," said Veronica, "as usual, just when it is getting interesting. Let's peek and see how many more columns we'll have. Let's make the sixth column for the laments over Babylon. Then the seventh column would be for the finishing of everything."

Helena was staring at the chart. Veronica waited, and waited some more. Finally Helena spoke. "Do you remember how some of the monks from which we read made the reading from beginning to end of the Apocalypse about the history of the church, and some of them made each set of seven be about that history. Do you see what we have here? We do see a sort of culminating stage at the last of every seven, and we also see culminating scenes at the end of the book. I wonder how those two views work together."

"Well, if you start in chapter 1 with the apostles and see chapter 22 as the final settling of God's kingdom, then the main problem is to determine where we are in the consecutive reading. If I remember right, some scholars had us at chapter 16, and some at chapter 20. What if I think we're earlier in the narrative?" said Veronica as they put away the books and paper and ink, and continued to think.

That evening they learned that Katharina had married Martin Luther (13 June 1525), the professor who had helped the girls escape the cloister (4 April 1523), and the one who had spoken and written both against the

Roman Church, with its large-scale selling of forgiveness, and against some not Christlike actions by some clergy.

"Isn't Martin Luther the one who doesn't like the Apocalypse because he can see no grace in it?" Helena asked. "What about you, Veronica? I see and feel Jesus all through the Apocalypse, and much grace."

"Well, I think this Luther thinks we're living in the last days, so maybe he will read the Apocalypse some more," said Veronica. "I hear he thinks the Pope, or rather the whole church system built up around the Pope, is the Antichrist."

"We did see hints of that in our reading, didn't we," said Helena. "When can we go again to work on our Apocalypse project?"

TIME OF UNITED STATES EXPANSION, 1791–1861[5]

Cheryl Shipman sat quietly. She'd been nervous, excited, and busy for the last fortnight, but today she listened calmly to Madame Archambeau's voice telling more stories of the French Revolution. She sat for this elderly French lady who had been young in the revolution and kept her youth by telling stories.

Cheryl's father, Charles Shipman, was home from sea this week. It was because of his sea captain notoriety that she had so many opportunities to know things. He had met Joseph Wolf on Wolf's travels as "missionary to the world," and was impressed with Wolf's sure confidence that Jesus would return to earth soon.

Cheryl's father loved books, and often brought some home to her. He made book exchanges all over the world and supplied many private libraries in the United States. Though ninety-five colleges had been founded since the first one, Harvard, in the United States, many of the best libraries were still the private ones, fed by book lovers like Charles Shipman.

Cheryl Shipman had read Homer, Dante, Milton, Bunyan, and all of Edward Gibbon's *Decline and Fall of the Roman Empire*. Most of all, she read Revelation and Daniel. She made the parallel columns as others before her had done and was able to add church history dates for the seven churches (Rev 2–3) and the seven seals (Rev 6–7). The seven trumpets (Rev 8–9) seemed to fall into place as she read Gibbon about the Roman Empire. She added dates there, too, for Alaric the Goth, Genseric the Vandal, Atilla the Hun, and Odoacer the Herulian.

---

5. My research for these stories included "Bible Societies"; D'Aubigne, *History of the Reformation*; De Tocqueville, *Old Regime and the Revolution*; "Founding Dates of States."

Madame Archambeau was saying, "You know there was a Roman Catholic Revival just as there was a Protestant Reformation, don't you?" Cheryl had heard these stories before, and today it was good to hear them again.

"Remind me of how that happened while I fix us a little lunch," said Cheryl.

"There was so much interest in Revelation, even calling the Pope the antichrist," continued Madame Archambeau, "that the Revival, already going on in the Roman Catholic Church since the Council of Trent in 1545, went in two different directions. The Jesuit Francisco Ribera creatively enlarged the idea that most of Revelation will happen in the distant future, beyond this age, so the antichrist really doesn't concern us. You've kept up with some of the travels and preaching John Darby, who greatly popularized this story, haven't you?"

"Yes," said Cheryl, setting out some sandwiches and herbal tea.

Madame Archambeau went on. "The Jesuit Louis de Alcazar built on the ideas of Porphyry to assure readers that these things have already taken place in the distant past. However, you and I have come to believe that there is a compelling story in Revelation and Daniel that arches over all of history from the prophet's time to the coming of Jesus again to this earth."

"Oh, I say there must have been some part of the story that intrigued the first readers long ago," said Cheryl. "And yes, the overarching story is the one that intrigues me most now. We are the privileged ones to see it come to fruition. Come, Madame, let's eat a bit to keep up your strength."

Madame Archambeau didn't stop to eat though she nibbled as she talked. "I brought that up about the Roman Catholic Revival because I wanted us to review what the various nations did with the Reformation. Germany produced the Protest of the Princes, the beginning of the Protestant faith. England produced the American colonies and John Darby with popular futurism. Spain just kept on with the Roman Catholic Inquisition. France made a revolution.

"I was there. I had such hopes," she said. "We had astonishing love and generosity for each other. We were a team, all of us, and we were going to save the world. We took out the government, the social structures, and the church. Now in hindsight, I know that no one else had ever before taken out all three at the same time. We were thorough, but we had no plan. My friends and I could clear the lot, but we couldn't build anything really new." Madame Archambeau was crying now, for her friends who had never found a loving God after that.

Cheryl cleaned and put away the few dishes and utensils. Then she sat down beside her charge and held the older lady's hand to cheer her and give her strength.

"It is helpful to me when you tell me of those days," Cheryl said. "I think I can almost see Rev 11 in your French Revolution. The Bible, the Old and New Testaments, the witnesses of God were dead in the streets, with partying all around, people glad that God is dead. Then Rev 11 indicates that the witnesses will rise again. And how! Review with me the ways. It will cheer you."

"Bible Societies are founded in Britain, Switzerland, Germany, Holland, Norway, America, and even Paris, in 1818. The Bible has been translated into every major language in the world with more dialect translations being added weekly. Truly the Bible rose again," said Cheryl.

"Ours wasn't the only revolution," continued Madame Archambeau. "When I heard of the American Revolution at age ten, my heart leapt for joy. I could feel the new vitality in my family. As I grew, I heard more about people in the United States making their own laws with checks and balances on the offices, and about how they kept religion out from under government control. This made me happy, but alas, we couldn't reproduce it. We had killed God."

Cheryl reminded them of two great awakenings, the one in England with Charles and John Wesley, and the later one in America with Charles Grandison Finney and lots of camp meetings. "Remember Cane Ridge camp meeting," she smiled. "You had just arrived from France and what a shock we were to you! That camp meeting was the place where I received such a large love for Jesus. I really can hardly wait to see him."

A little impatience was creeping into the room, though the two of them worked hard at cheering one another through the afternoon. Father came down for supper. They didn't eat much. He retold the story for them of how he had met Joseph Bates, another sea captain, retired.

"He told us of the calculations from Daniel's time in about 500 BCE, stretching 2300 years until now. How thrilling that was, just as if we'd been given the coordinates for a treasure at sea. And then he told us of this little-known treaty in the Middle East that happened on August 11, 1840, exactly as understood, ten days prior, by Bates's friends in studying the prophecies. That was another thrill like seeing a small island exactly where we expected it in the middle of the sea."

"Oh, I love Jesus so much," said Cheryl, coming back from the window. She could hardly sit still now. "God gave us the Bible so we could know God. Then God gave us the prophecies so we could know God better. I so long for Jesus to come so we can know God better yet."

It was getting dark outside. They had three hours to wait. Of course, it might not be that long.

Since none of them could remember that far back, it was Madame Archambeau who brought up the earthquake in Lisbon in 1955, that reached a greater distance than any earthquake before it, so people thought it was a sign.

"Then there was the dark day in 1980 in New England when the sun went dark and the moon went red and chickens went to roost in midday, another sign," said Cheryl.

Father said, "Joseph Bates told me that the Great Leonid Storm in 1833 had people crying in the streets thinking the end had come. He said this is what caught his attention to turn his life around."

Thirty minutes were left in October 22, 1844. Many around the world expected Jesus to come about this time. Some in the United States were convinced it would be this day. Let us not roast or ridicule them. Let us try to understand, and let our hearts be melted for them, in their love and commitment to the living Christ who would surely fulfill their longing to see him.

At fifteen minutes to midnight. Cheryl reached for the hands of her fellow watchers. They were quiet now. Five minutes. Two. One.

The wail that arose at a few minutes after midnight on that sad night was like the midnight wail in Egypt in the homes where the angel had not passed them by. This night, the Lord seemed indeed to have passed them by.

Cheryl sobbed and sobbed. "I loved him," she cried over and over again.

Madame Archambeau put her out her hand and stroked the girl's hair. "Poor child," she said. "You have so little experience with disappointment yet."

Father mumbled prayers in his chair for a long time and then went out to the woodshed to do there what he had to do in conversation with God.

When the waterworks in the eyes were dry, and the energy all spent, Cheryl lay with her head in Madame Archambeau's lap. The sobbing caught her breath only once in a while now.

Then she said, "I need to read Revelation and Daniel some more. It's my place of solace. It is where I meet the living Christ."

TIME OF GLOBAL ADVANCEMENT, 2000-2022

Hello. I am June Kingston. I have asked for this audience, and I am grateful that you as leaders of this church, are here. There are too many here to handle a dialogue kind of presentation, so we will have questions and answers later.

It was probably forty years ago that I first realized the world's economic systems were all tied together to go bankrupt like dominoes when we can't prop up or bail out pieces anymore. Since then, we've had the digital boom and bust, the attack on the World Trade Center, the housing boom and bust, and the pandemic disruptions, all further intensifying the global nature of our economic system.

With the advent and expansion of the micro-blogging platforms like Facebook and Twitter beginning in 2004, I soon realized we already have a global IT system.

About the time of the Fukushima tsunami in 2011, I figured out that our water, air, and weather are shared globally. The global ecosystem has been in the news for decades now.

In the pandemic of 2019, I realized our health is already a global system.

Now I remember I've seen global social unrest, too, in riots, racism, migrations, and drug and sex trafficking.

We used to focus on fighting off a one-world government; now look around. It is here. It is us. Global financial, ecological, social, information, and health systems already exist. It is already set up. What's left are minor phases.

This is why I craved this audience to show you my work of many years. I'm compelled. Thank you for listening.

Revelation is compelling. I have five different approaches to, and results of, inductive reading of Revelation that I must show you, with some hints as to where they might lead. I hope others will pursue my research and inductive reading experiments.

One: Then-Stretch-Now

Throughout my research and observations, I have remained committed to maintain interest in the historical context of the writing, to explore how the first readers might have understood it at the time of its writing. This is the *"Then,"* and visually I think of it as the left leg of the capital letter *H*.

I also remain committed to an overarching meta-narrative of God's plan for earth and its redemption. With this in mind, I have researched, down through historical times, the interpretations of Revelation that were in use, that fit this historical mega-story. Historical events mark out the *"Stretch,"* and visually I think of it as the crossbar of a stretched capital letter *H*.

Further, I remain committed to finding the presence of Jesus Christ in Revelation. After all, it is called the Revelation of Jesus Christ. I expect lessons for today for me and my people granted us by the Holy Spirit sent from Christ's throne. I insist on harvesting lessons for today in the context of the earliest readers, in the words and scenes of the writing, in the historical happenings of the historicist interpretations, and in the patterns among them all. This is the *"Now,"* and visually I think of it as the right leg, after the stretch, of the capital letter *H*.

I propose that all these three, the *"Then,"* the *"Stretch,"* and the *"Now,"* belong to the historicist method[6] of interpretation. By the historicist method, we look at the origins of the writing, we look at applications in the stretch of history as many readers before us did, and we seek the promised blessing for ourselves now.

I am interested in the setting in which the prophecy was given, the *"Then,"* out of which the prophet pulled words and images by which to tell what he had seen. I am interested in the historical *"Stretch"* over which fulfillment of prophecy marched along. I am also interested in the spiritual blessing and guidance to be gleaned today from noticing the patterns in all of it and comparing them to what is happening *"Now."* I think it is beneficial to our spiritual lives to keep all these ideas and stories alive and growing as our *"Now"* marches onward toward the climax of history.

Let's take a break. Stand up, walk, look far away, breathe, wiggle. Then come back, please. I will give you five different approaches to reading Revelation inductively. I've given you one so far.

Two: Sevens Connect[7]

Welcome back from break. I'm June Kingston, and I'm here to give you five different approaches to reading Revelation inductively. This will be the second.

We'll turn our attention now to the sevens. As did so many before me, I started out in Revelation by making columns of the sets of seven. As did others, I noticed similarities across the columns. I noticed that the first four steps, or stages, of some of the sevens held elements that matched some in the first four steps of another seven. I documented what I saw and puzzled over the instances where I found no similarities in corresponding stages.

---

6. For easily accessible instances of the historicist method and comparison to the other methods, here are my recommendations: Paulien, *Deep Things of God*; Tucker, *Meeting Jesus*; Stefanovic, *Plain Revelation*; Vetne, *Jesus in the Book of Revelation*.

7. My research for this story included Anonymous, *Pearl Poet*.

There is so much more to understand, and these observations kept me coming back to Revelation to trace more and more ideas with Jesus.

I was in the habit of reading Daniel with Revelation. I noticed the similarities between the king's dream and Daniel's dream. Again, it is in the first four steps of the seven where the similarities are readily noticed. In this case the interpretation is given in the biblical text and a good case can be made that both dreams picture the same history and the same events as fulfillment. One dream recapitulates, and adds to, the other in prophesying the same historical events. Before long I had carried over, to Daniel from Revelation, the habit of making columns of sevens. I had carried over, to Revelation from Daniel, the habit of expecting one seven to recapitulate another.

Some readers of Revelation want this recapitulation among the sevens to indicate the concept that history repeats itself. Surely, we can learn much from the patterns in history, yet I do not let the replicating sevens indicate for me that history will continue always in endless cycles of repetition. Some of the sevens of Revelation and Daniel do obviously connect, and they show us that there is surely a climactic end of all the "cycles," directed by God.

Neither do these replicating sevens encourage me to look for multiple fulfillments of prophecy. It is the prophecy that is multiple, not the fulfillment.

There is much more to be noticed and thought through about the connections among the sevens. Additionally, there are other subplots made by other systematic similarities. There are orderly, itemized presentations of the furniture from the Hebrew and Jewish sanctuary and temple. There are interludes between the sevens that have similarities to each of the sevens on either side of them. Each set of seven has its own internal patterns of similarities. There are exciting similarities and differences to be researched between the Lamb and each of the two women who dominate the last half of Revelation. The possibilities seem endless for joyful inductive research with the risen Christ in Revelation.

We used to be careful to limit possible interpretations of a writing to what the human author could have imagined and intended in his writing. More recently, scholars have recognized that none of us can know for sure a dead author's intention.[8] Instead, for confidence in reading, we need to build live communities of inductive reading, and also apply ourselves to the author's own work for clues to authorial intention..

Further, I think I need to be careful lest I allow my own limitations to limit what I think another artist-author could have imagined and pulled

---

8. Hayes and Holladay, *Biblical Exegesis*, 168.

together. In expanding my expectations, I came across a poem created in about 1400 by an anonymous poet. The poem is called "Pearl," and demonstrates so many different patterns of rhyme, alliteration, and repetition as to astound the senses and overwhelm the counting of the patterns. At the same time, the story material is deep and rich and magnificently told. Other poems from that era use some of the same skills, but this one outshines the others. I choose not to confine John to the limits of my own abilities of imagination and intention.

The sevens connect and show a many-faceted, climactic ending to the over-arching story.

I came here to describe five different approaches for inductive research in Revelation. I've given you two so far.

Three: Dan 7 and Rev 13 Connect

Looking for sevens whose steps contain multiple similarities so as to render them parallel sevens, my attention landed on Dan 7 and Rev 13. Between these two chapters I found four significantly identical phrases besides the same order of listing of four identically named animals. (My work was with the *Septuagint*,[9] the Greek translation of the Old Testament, and the *United Bible Society Greek New Testament*,[10] noting significance only with three or more main words replicated in identical order.[11]) Since these two chapters are thus thoroughly connected and lie at the physical center of their books, it seemed to me that the two books are thoroughly connected at their centers. Further I discovered that if I expand the view to look at Rev 12–14 as the central section, there are three more significantly identical phrases, matching Dan 7. (See Appendix 1: "Verbal Parallels between Daniel and Revelation.")

Curious creature that I am, I looked around to see if there are other connections between the two books. What I found was that Revelation and Daniel are replete with identical key words, themes, and scenes, not sprinkled around randomly, but marching through the two books like ties connecting the rails. (See Appendix 2: "Scene and Theme Parallels between Daniel and Revelation.")

This thrills me because when Joseph was called to interpret two dreams that had similarities, his comment about why there were two was that the

---

9. *Septuagint with Apocrypha.*

10. Aland et al., *Greek New Testament.*

11. My research and notations were influenced and shaped by Beale, *John's Use of the Old Testament*; Beale, *Use of Daniel.*

doubling shows the divine plan they represented as sure and imminent (Gen 41:32). Since I noticed this doubling in Revelation and Daniel, I have been continually energized by the possibilities of its meanings.

Someone asks me how I think that happened. Well, of course I can't know the intentions of either of these dead authors. Yet I can imagine John being very familiar with the book of Daniel and perhaps letting it guide his own organization of material. After all, both Daniel and John were exiles having experienced the sacking of their city, Jerusalem, and its temple. Besides, Jesus had encouraged John to read and understand Daniel (Matt 24:15).

Further, it was a Hebrew habit to re-tell stories with imagination for the issues of the present. Evidence of this lies in the many repetitions of the story of creation and the story of the deliverance from Egypt. Another example of retelling in a creative way is in Jeremiah's use of David's Ps 1 (Jer 17:5–10). The parallel nature of the two writings is obvious though there are creative changes for the then-current situation.

The doubling of the dream, Revelation matching Daniel in many ways, could have happened because of the similar circumstances of the writers, because of John's familiarity with Daniel, and because it was a habit of Hebrew thought to follow patterns in previous works when creating new ones.

There are connections between Dan 7 and Rev 13 and, in turn, these chapters connect their two books to show their stories are sure and imminent.

Let's take another break. Stand up, walk, look far away, breathe, wiggle. Then come back, please. This has been the third of five approaches to reading Revelation inductively.

Four: Chiasm Identifies Center

Welcome back from break. I'm June Kingston, and I'm here to give you five different approaches to reading Revelation inductively. This will be the fourth.

"*Chi*" is the Greek alphabetical letter that looks like an *X*. The word "chiasm" simply means mirror image, envelope-within-envelope construction, nesting dolls, or always coming full circle. Through counting Greek words and making mistakes and false starts, I gathered significant verbal evidence of chiastic construction in Revelation. Chapters 21–22 match chapters 1–3, chapters 19–20 match chapters 4–7, chapters 17–18 match chapter 6, chapters 15–16 match chapters 8–11, and chapter 14 matches chapter 12. This "match" is by significantly identical phrases in significant density in both locations.

Noticing chiastic structure does two things for my walk with the living Christ in Revelation.

First, noticing the chiastic structure gives me a building sense of closure and satisfactory finish, climaxing at the end. All the loose ends have been tied up, all open circuits closed, all arguments answered. This is a mental health benefit built right into the structure of Revelation, available for our healing.

Second, noticing the chiastic structure identifies the center of the book. The chiastic center of the writing points out for me the place where we are, sort of hanging out until all other things get ready to start turning backwards. We've been carrying on our lives in the fold of history, a wrinkle in time, in Rev 12–14. There is much more that can be gained in insights and blessings from those three chapters if read as our home plate for right now.

Further, there are verbal indications that prophecies will fulfill much more quickly in the last half of the chiasm than they did in the first. I believe we can expect immense upheaval when history turns back on itself. Creation will start to be undone, with unquenchable fires, unbounded seas, untreatable diseases, unstoppable miscarriages, unmitigated depression, and more.

Chiasm identifies the center and shows us we are living in the fold of history, the wrinkle in time. Let us research and communicate.

I've now given you four of five different approaches to reading Revelation and Daniel inductively.

Five: Two Parallel Books Make a Plot

It really is a story. The whole big picture of Revelation and Daniel is a story with plot and characters, with beginning, thickening, solution, resolution, and closure. Through innumerable times reading the two books, I have always stalked the plot only to be caught up in it and come to the end of the reading with joy and the desire to read it again.

I am not the first who has wondered at the big story and thought it must have something to do with the walk of the church through history. Though it is not at all so evident to me how dates and events might fit in the whole plot, as it is in the other approaches I have presented here, still there is much to learn. I believe experiencing the story plot while reading

Revelation and Daniel actually teaches us the way God is at work in the cosmic conflict.

What I know right now is that God waits for Satan to make a bold move and then God uses that disruption in history to further God's way. And God's working all things to God's glory is never puny, or negligible. When God takes advantage of an advance by Satan, God bursts open the treasure house of heaven to win the allegiance of kings, or to send his gospel everywhere to everyone, or to let the fickle power-alliances of the evil one break up and be exposed.

We have read to the end of the book, and we know how God wins.

I have shown you five approaches to Revelation and Daniel that I think are important for now and for inductive reading. Now let me close.

Here is my conclusion. My friends, I believe we are all set to leave the fold of history. We used to oppose a one-world government because we saw in Revelation what a one-world government can do against God. I tell you we passed that milepost a long time ago. We are global, economically, ecologically, socially, informationally, and medically.

What concerns me more is if we are global without God. American Christians complain about taking payer out of our schools, the Ten Commandments out of our courtrooms, and nativity scenes out of our town squares. Yet did we not already acquiesce to taking God out of the creation of this world, taking God out of the origins of the Bible, and now will we also acquiesce to plans to make peace and security on this planet without thought of God?

Will we not enter most seriously into prayer that God himself will be present in the meeting rooms where new governments and their policies are forged, and that the results may be at least as brilliant for our time as the United States Constitution was for its time? Will we not let our prayers grow exponentially, the same way technology grows, that we ourselves will be kept from entertaining coercion by fear, shame, guilt, or violence, and that all peoples may be free? Will we not ask God to make his presence and guidance felt in planning rooms, either virtual or in-person spaces, where activists develop ways of creating momentum in society? Will we not pray for the peace of the globe?

I believe the only salvation for the human race and its earth lies in Jesus Christ who wants to reveal himself in the book of Revelation to individuals all over this earth. It's time to declare our belief in God without trying to coerce others to our way. It's time to read the Bible for ourselves and pray together and apart. It's time to create local communities with colleagues and connections who are determined to rely on God and read Revelation inductively together.

I have said what I came here to say. I'm June Kingston, and I thank you for your attention to my work with five different approaches to reading Revelation inductively.

Questions are welcome.

2

Lessons from the Sevens

INTRODUCTION: REASONS FOR SEVEN[1]

What sevens have been meaningful to you? Age seven? Age seventy-seven? Seventh day? Seven years? Seventh grade? Other? Where are sevens used today?

There are many sevens in the book of Revelation. We will spend a few sessions here exploring the instances of seven where there is a series of seven events or images. We will not tackle the instances of seven where the word seven is only descriptive and not introducing a series. Other sevens in Revelation include, lampstands, stars, spirits, burning lamps, horns, eyes, thunders, heads, crown, angels, mountains, and kings. Each of these invites more research.

We can start out with recognizing that the number seven in the Bible indicates completeness, finish, enough, or rest, so recognized from the story

---

1. My research for these thoughts on the sevens included at least the following resources: Beale, *Book of Revelation*; Beale, *John's Use of the Old Testament*; Beale, *Use of Daniel*; Boring, *Revelation*; Collins, *Apocalypse*; Collins, *Apocalyptic Imagination*; Doukhan, *Secrets of Daniel*; Doukhan, *Secrets of Revelation*; Fiorenza, *Book of Revelation*; Fiorenza, *Revelation*; Koester, *Revelation and the End*; Paulien, *Deep Things of God*; Paulien, *Gospel from Patmos*; Peterson, *Reversed Thunder*; Reis, *Echoes of the Most Holy*; Richard, *Apocalypse*; Rowland, *Radical Christianity*; Stefanovic, *Plain Revelation*; Stefanovic, *Revelation of Jesus Christ*; Stefanovic, *Daniel, Wisdom to the Wise*; Tonstad, *Revelation*; Tucker, *Meeting Jesus*; Vetne, *Jesus in the Book of Revelation*; Wainwright, *Mysterious Apocalypse*.

of Creation in the first and second chapters of Genesis. If you can join me in seeing the number seven as linked to creation week, then what do you think the number six might mean? I offer the idea that six is the number of humans. Six is the last number before finish, the sign of something yet lacking. As we study these sevens, I suggest examining the sixth step in each series of seven, asking, What are the similarities and differences among the sixth stages?

Many of the sevens are clearly grouped as four plus three. We might look for the similarities and differences among the sevens in view of the fours and the threes. I notice that often the first four are more clearly delineated than are the last three. I wonder if this might be to leave God a little room at the end of each seven to work in mysterious ways.

Besides all these enticing trails to follow, we will attempt to look at each seven with the three different modes: *"Then," "Stretch,"* and *"Now."*

In this book the *"Then"* is not packed away somewhere in the un-presuming past, but is the anchor to the prophecy. *"Then"* is not a fulfillment of that prophecy, but the setting out of which the prophecy was stated. You can find this historical setting by searching the Internet on the key words. I will not spend much time on this history here. The preterist school of thought and interpretation would see in this historical setting the whole authorial incentive and intention for the writing. I intend to cast this historical setting as merely the fertile soil for appreciation of the prophecy in which this appreciation and valuation took root and protected the writing for future generations.

I use the term *"Stretch"* to indicate the overarching mega-story, from outset to denouement. You can find the historicist interpretation of Revelation by searching Wikipedia on merely "historicist" plus "Revelation." I will not spend many words here on identifying or describing this march through the historical ages.

The "historicist method" of interpretation, with its derivative "historicism," as I have seen it in practice, holds room for the full scope of Revelation from before the world was made,[2] as well as for attention to each, the *"Then,"* the *"Stretch,"* and the *"Now,"* as I describe them here.

Here are other words that might help explain, by their correlation, what I mean. My *"Then"* would include "exegesis" and "archaeology." My *"Now"* would include "soteriology," "theology," "ecclesiology," "homiletics," and simply "relationships." My *"Stretch"* would include all of Revelation's scope from the distant past, through historical existence as we know it, and

---

2 For easily accessible instances of the historicist method and comparison to the other methods, here are my recommendations: Paulien, *Deep Things of God*; Tucker, *Meeting Jesus*; Stefanovic, *Plain Revelation*; Vetne, *Jesus in the Book of Revelation*.

into the distant future, otherwise called "the great controversy" or "cosmic conflict."

All these, when applied to Revelation, are comprehended in the term "historicism," as I have known it. If a reader thinks I have gone off into preterism, idealism, or futurism, I attest that I reject the limitations often placed on the scope represented by those words and those who claim them. I believe that the scope of Revelation is cosmic, with never a time, since Daniel at least, that is not covered by prophecy.

We have examined how the *"Then"* and the *"Stretch"* will work here. Next, I will explain how the *"Now"* will work.

In this book, the *"Now"* is not shuffled off to some far distant future but is the current vitality of the prophecy. *"Now"* is not a fulfillment of that prophecy, but lessons for today from history, either history *"Then"* or history in the *"Stretch."* I will spend more time and words on the *"Now."* I will use imagination with inductive reading. This is not to define an interpretation in order to offer it as "truth" or as "fulfillment of prophecy." This is to explore lessons that could be taken to heart from reviewing centuries of Christian work with the Revelation of the living Jesus Christ.

It is for this Jesus Christ that I write and offer praises. "Unto him who loved us and washed us from our sins in his own blood and has made us kings and priests to God and his Father—to him be glory and dominion for ever and ever" (Rev 1:5-6 KJV, WZ paraphrase). I find the greatest happiness in recognizing, every day before my Lord, my sins and need of washing, which recognition is my most sure tutor into his love and good future.

The book you are reading now is merely a guide showing you expansions and summaries that I have loved in reading Revelation inductively. You might find in this little guide ways that Revelation could teach you how to deal with conflict in your church or your home, how to start a business or an organization, and how to keep it vibrant; how to survive when the whole system gets riddled with anxiety; how to avoid taking up, or getting taken up in, fear, shame, and guilt; or how to build love, acceptance, and forgiveness into your organization or project. You will find adventure and help in *The Happiest Book I Ever Read*.

I hope you are persuaded to get a composition book now and write your observations as you read Revelation and Daniel. First hint: Copy down in your own words the first praise piece that you find and add to the praise words as you continue through the book of Revelation.

SEVEN CHURCHES[3]

For good foundation in the *"Then"* of the seven churches (Rev 2–3), please research what was each city's history, culture, religion, and reputation. You can do this on the Internet, or in a good pictorial Bible dictionary.[4] I will add one observation. The fourth letter, the middle one, the one to the church in Thyatira, is the longest and holds the most description of trouble in the church. The introduction of the sender, the return address or letterhead, if you will, calls him Son of God. This is the only place in the whole book of Revelation where he is so identified. Of the designated cities of the addressee churches, Thyatira was the most commercially tied to Rome. In Rome, the current emperor was considered the son of god, since Julius Caesar had been voted, in senate session, to be "God." I wonder if the readers in Thyatira were shocked, pleased, grateful, or fearful to be called out as receiving a letter from the real Son of God.

For the *"Stretch,"* please also check out historicist interpretations of the seven churches on the Internet. The timeline we have been using, with the notation of the churches added, gives a visual approximation of the usual historicist interpretation. The dates are all approximate.

Seven Churches

Date	Event	Church
1000	Adam	
600	Noah	
500	Abraham	
300	Moses	
0	David	
100	Daniel, Babylon	
300	Esther, Persia	
500	Antiochus IV Epiphanes, Greece	Ephesus
700	Jesus, Rome	Smyrna
1000	John	Pergamum
1500	Constantine	Thyatira
1800	Pope Gregory I	
2000	Islamic Advancement	
	Pope Gregory VII	Sardis
	Martin Luther	Philadelphia
	United States Expansion	Laodicea
	Global Advancement	

---

3. My research for the interpersonal communication aspects of my comments on the seven churches included these resources: Augsburger, *Caring Enough to Confront*; Augsburger, *Caring Enough to Forgive*; Augsburger, *Caring Enough to Hear*; Elgin, *Gentle Art of Verbal Self-Defense*; Evans, *Controlling People*; Evans, *Verbally Abusive Relationship*; Friedman, *Generation to Generation*; Goulston, *Just Listen*; Haugk, *Antagonists in the Church*.

4. For good pictorial and historical help, I recommend Wilson, *Revelation*.

There are many lessons for the *"Now"* that could be drawn from each of the letters to the seven churches. I proffer here a series of seven lessons for *"Now"* that focus on communication, interpersonal, small group communication. The churches were small groups to which Jesus Christ sent letters about how to improve their group life and fellowship. I work on the premise that families and some churches and corporations are small groups in which we would like to have improved group life and fellowship. I will present here my understanding from the seven letters to the seven small churches, as to how to improve interpersonal and small group communication.

Furthermore, the letters Jesus Christ sent to these seven churches appear as if dictated by Jesus himself and taken down as Jesus spoke them. Because of this, I feel invited to study and teach the communication skills manifested in these letters as those of the living Jesus Christ himself.

Let us observe the packaging of messages in the letters. After the address and the return address, the first sentence of the body of the letters begins with "I know . . ." and usually describes something positive about the addressee. Then comes the negative evaluation and what to do about it. After that Jesus returns to the positive with a beautiful promise crafted especially with that addressee in mind. The sign-off is the same in each letter, "Let whoever has ears hear what the Spirit says to the churches" (Rev 2:7 KJV, WZ paraphrase). I notice that the negative evaluation and the corrective measures come sandwiched between some very positive pieces. This is a good way to communicate: use twice as much positive as negative and say the positive before and after the negative.

I mentioned the fact that the body of the letter begins with the words, "I know . . ." and follows with some very astute observations which would have required careful and lengthy listening to gain. Apparently, Jesus listens. Perhaps you have noticed that, when someone listens to you and really gets what you are committed to or fearful about, you feel validated in your worth as a person, you feel a small bit of inner healing. This is the power of the gift of attentive, respectful listening, the gift of calm presence. Jesus demonstrated this in his time on this earth.

If we were to count the number of times Jesus says "I" in these letters, we might be astounded and wonder how we do not hear him as conceited and selfish. Saying "I" can be one of the most humble and vulnerable ways to be in communication. Saying "I" leads to powerful communication because each of us can know this topic best and stand most clearly and firmly on the related information.

Now let us examine the churches in order. At first, the church in Ephesus was white-hot in devotion and love (see Acts 19). With the influx of diverse new group members, however, it had trouble accepting some of the new ones in the same kind of love (Eph 4:2, 15–16, 31–32). Jesus told them they had left their first love and they needed to repent and act like they did at first. I read here what to do when facing simple diversity. Rather than closing off the different new person, I can speak my truth in love, listen to the other respectfully, laugh together about our differences, and reassign tasks and boundaries according to our different gifts and preferences.

Smyrna (modern Izmir) had a history of being bullied and snubbed, its people being victims of slander and deceit. There are situations where the other persons seem to have no care to be kind in communication. I may face bullying in various forms: gossip, pressure to conform, unfair competition, and lying. It may seem that my confusion is the other person's goal. Jesus said to Smyrna, "Don't be afraid; be faithful" (Rev 2:20 KJV, WZ paraphrase). Jesus says to me, "Don't react; just repeat your request or truth and agree with what you can."

Pergamum was in competition with Alexandria to have the largest ancient library. Then Alexandria cut off papyrus supplies, so Pergamum invented parchment. I may find myself in direct open conflict with others for the same resources or spaces. I may find others blaming, name-calling, or becoming violent. Jesus said one problem in Pergamum is that people try to cause others to stumble in order to gain advantage. In open conflict, both sides must each repent and own our fault, then use the sword Jesus offers to find our clarity, our bottom line, and stop insisting on getting more than necessary for each.

Thyatira was a center of textile production and sales, the source of the colors of royalty (see Acts 16:14). Thyatira was a place of increasing dependence on trade, rising consumption, and economic corruption, a place where boundaries got blurred and people controlled other people. Sometimes in communication I can feel the anxiety of the system based on fear, shame, and guilt. I may feel blamed or ignored, used or confused, or pushed to extremes. I may not be able to penetrate to understand motives or who is motivating. Yet I can say what I stand for, I can ask for "I" language around me, and I can choose intentional calm presence rather than reacting. Jesus says, "I'll ask nothing more of you. Hold onto what you have" (Rev 2:24–25 KJV, WZ paraphrase).

Sardis perched on the top of a steep mountain, virtually impregnable to enemy attack, and claimed fame by its cemetery of famous people from years gone by. It reminds me of communication situations where the attack gets in close and personal. Personal secrets, push-button words, spiking decibels, and accusing presuppositions are the flags of verbal abuse. Jesus says, "Watch and strengthen what is weak" (Rev 3:2 KJV, WZ paraphrase). In Jesus I can strengthen my weak confidence. I can remember who I am and hold my person close. Jesus says, "Repent." I can practice not raising my voice and not reacting to accusations. I can learn to recognize the hook that draws me in, and I can choose to speak my truth against that hook in calm non-reactivity.

Philadelphia was the city of brotherly love—not *storge*, which is familial familiar love; not *eros*, which is lovers' love; but *philia*, which is friend love. Though earthquakes and enemies tried to level this city, its people refused to give up their community love. Yet there were some who wanted to destroy it. I can get into communication situations where it seems that someone wants to destroy me and all I have built. They lie and bring barbed jokes and unkind "news." They ask trick questions and use vicious language. I can walk away from the bait, the challenge, the argument, the putdown. I can maintain my non-reactivity, keeping a smile in my eyes and love in my heart for the other person, as I leave. Jesus says, "Look, I have opened a door for you" (Rev 3:8 KJV, WZ paraphrase).

Laodicea was the city of self-help, who refused empire help in rebuilding after the earthquake. Laodicea boasted of its own physicians and mineral springs, a famous salve for healing eyesight, and sheep who grew black wool. Jesus said they needed him. I can get into the mode of thinking that I have conquered all communication hurdles, or at least now I have all the tools for every situation. I may think I can, or ought to be able to, fix any part of my life for myself. Jesus says, "No, you can't fix your life and communication without me. Please notice that you are poor, blind, naked, and will be ashamed. I'm knocking at your door. I can take care of you. Will you let me in?" (Rev 3:17–20 KJV, WZ paraphrase).

In the letters to the seven churches, God has given us marvelous instruction, as well as delightful promises, for those who use these methods to succeed in Christlike communication. One of the most important baseline methods is to let the living Jesus in as he knocks by the Holy Spirit.

SEVEN SEALS[5]

"Then." The seven seals (Rev 6–7) would have captured the attention of the first readers because Roman seals are ubiquitous in the artifacts of the time. Seals showed authority. The authorized person might carry the seal as a finger ring, an amulet for bracelet or necklace, or a goblet or block carefully protected. The mark of the seal might show up on coins, on letters and documents, on doorways and other architecture, or on tombs.

5. My research on my organizational life cycle comments on the seven seals included Hamm, *Recreating the Church*.

You can search the Internet for more about seals, horses, portents, and other items you find in the seven seals.

"Stretch." Only Jesus, the Lamb, could open the history on the progress and troubles of the church down through the ages. Only Jesus has the authority to break the seals and open the book (Rev 4–5). An overarching historicist view of the seven seals would see them as picturing the fortunes of the church from John's day to the end, and match their dates as somewhat similar to those of the seven churches. For the sixth seal, many using the historicist view would point to the Great Lisbon Earthquake in 1755, the New England Dark Day and dull Moon in 1780, and the Leonid Meteor Storm in 1833.

"Now." If Jesus could open the book on the life cycle of the church, perhaps he can open the book to help us understand the life cycle of our churches, our businesses, our projects, or even our marriages and families. I am not showing a new interpretation of the seven seals. I am simply learning some lessons from the brand-new venture that was the Christian church to help us let the living Christ into our current new ventures. I suggest that the life cycles of our ventures are similar to the life cycle of the church through the ages, and that we and our ventures can benefit from reading the seven seals inductively.

What games do you play that require some sort of password or permission to move from one level to the next? How does it feel to get that password each time? The seven seals are sort of like getting the password in order to go to the next level in your new venture.

Before we observe the opening of the seals, let us notice what this Jesus did in order to be the one qualified to open up our lives and ventures. One of the glorious bursts of praise just before the opening of the seals points to Jesus, "You are worthy to take the book, and open the seals, because you were killed and used your blood to redeem us to God" (Rev 5:9 KJV, WZ paraphrase). It looks like Jesus's venture to earth, to get us, depended on his dying. I would suggest there is a certain amount of humility or death to our own ego and arrogance that needs to come in and fill our ventures for him.

The opening of the first seal releases the venture. The white horse goes out conquering. I see it. Your venture is a vision. Your business will fill a gap in good. Your church ministry will help heal the world's ills. Your marriage will last forever, bless the world, and make happy, well-adjusted children. The rider on the white horse is given a crown, as your venture receives the green light and accolades from your fellows.

The opening of the second seal shows a red horse with rider going out killing. I have felt it. Our dreams feel the killing chill of red tape, red ink, red eyes. The testing of the venture must happen. Our business must have permits. Our church ministry meets resistance from powerful people. Our marriage has its first big flaring argument, and then some more. The rider on the red horse is given a sharp sword. We are given the Bible, sharper than any two-edged sword (Heb 4:12), by which to figure out how to cut the red tape, change the red ink, and heal the red eyes.

The opening of the third seal shows a black horse with a rider carrying a pair of balances, supposedly to weigh out merchandise and its payments. Here is how the black horse may show up. Our venture finally pulls up into the black ink. We have worked hard to formulate agreements, policies, structures, and even habits to meet all the requirements and obstacles. Our business hired a tax specialist. Our church ministry found the right powerful people for support. Our marriage settled on roles and spaces and procedures and got a couple children started. We can rock along now, doing what we were meant to do. Then we realize that the gap in good still exists, as do also the world's ills, and making happy, well-adjusted children is a job much more intense than we had ever expected. The rider on the black horse is given inflation and riches. The struggle continues in efforts to keep the successful venture successful.

The opening of the fourth seal shows a pale horse with a rider, dying. It seems to me that this could picture the stage when the venture must be kept alive at the cost of relationships or spirituality or physical health. The dream has grown cold, and the mere survival of the enterprise is what drives us now. The all-consuming goal is to keep our employees from joining the jobless statistics. The goal is to keep the ministry going because it is the only thing for which the church is known. The goal is merely to keep the family together, at least until the children finish high school. We bail out the ventures that are too large to fail, and we let many smaller ventures take the fall. We let some corporations consume smaller ventures and soon rule the field. Nations and world organizations lose their white-hot vision. The rider on the pale horse was given wars, starvation, plagues, and vicious animals (maybe merely rats as in the bubonic plague). We are given stress, anxiety, allergies, indigestion, irritableness, pollution, resistant illnesses, epidemics, etc.

The opening of the fifth seal shows people under the altar where they had been thrown as trash after they had been martyred for their faith. They cry out to God, "How long? How long before you will judge in righteousness?" (Rev 6:10 KJV, WZ paraphrase). In the overall life cycle of our ventures, perhaps these are those for whom the many venturers have been too busy, or those who wanted to be a part of the ventures but were marginalized. These are the people who were not the right kind to serve or be served in our church ministries. These are the children who were not tall enough to make us know their dreams at our great heights and amidst our great concerns. They are given white clothing and told to rest a little while because there are more to join them. Our ventures can turn around, can be revitalized if we can listen to those voices. Listen to those who have been hurt by our agreements, policies, structures, and even our habits. We needed to create the policies and structures to get us through; however, policies and structures are not the reason for our ventures' existence. If we will listen to the voices of those who have been hurt, perhaps we can turn our ventures around.

The opening of the sixth seal shows nature signing. Creation groans, waiting for God to make everything right (Rom 8:22). Nature is one of those who have been hurt by the policies and procedures created for the merely financial success of thousands of ventures.

In the opening of the seventh seal, everything is quiet. There are no more voices crying for justice, no more birds' sounds, not even any more industrious sounds of people in venture. Maybe that is a doomsday ending not really here yet. Maybe we have an opportunity to turn it around. In the silence a strange thing happens. An angel throws burning incense on the earth, incense representing the prayers of God's people. Some say this signifies an end of angelic support for opportunity, and I think that perhaps all the ventures, large and small, that failed in their mission might meet some sort of doom. It does not mean that prayers from individuals on earth are no longer effective, or that Jesus has stopped caring. In fact, it might picture the prayers scattering and spreading over earth for a new and greater connection between heaven and earth.

In the openings of the seven seals, God has given us a roadmap of adventure, and the tools we will need at each stage in any ventures' life cycle. Increased prayer would be an important tool.

SEVEN TRUMPETS[6]

"Then." The seven trumpets (Rev 8–11) appear in a part of the book of Revelation that matches Dan 5, which is a biblical account of the last night, the night of the fall of Babylon in 538 BCE. We think the Christians in John's time were used to calling the Roman Empire by the name Babylon (1 Pet 5:13), whether as a secret code or as a reminder not to fraternize with Rome. It seems to me that these early Christians could have seen in the trumpets the demise of something, and maybe they hoped it would be the demise of Rome.

You can find on the Internet information about the use of various kinds of trumpets, both in Rome and in Jerusalem.

---

6. My research on the environmental troubles in our world that I find reflected in the trumpets included Schwab and Malleret, *Great Narrative*; United Nations, "Transforming Our World."

Let us examine the first scene in Rev 8, which finishes the seals and begins the trumpets. This is where I propose we will find the living Jesus in the trumpets. He is called an angel, and he stands at the altar of incense with an incense burner in his hand. He is given much incense to burn and produce smoke to ascend with the prayers of God's people. I believe the first readers would have pictured Jesus at this place of intercession (Heb 7:25). Since calling God the "angel of the Lord" was common in Hebrew history (Gen 16:7–11; 22:11–15; Exod 3:2; Num 22:22–35; Judg 2:1–4; 6:11–21), Jesus as the Son of God, appearing as an angel, would not have been surprising.

People worry about the incense being thrown down to earth, and there are several possibilities about how the first readers might have viewed this. First, it might have seemed ominous, that Jesus's intercession is finished for the world's organizations who will not stop their oppressions. Second, it might have seemed bright, in that Jesus's prayers now go up from earth, more intimately tied with his people's prayers. Third it might have interested them as simply a dramatic gesture to capture the attention of the universe. At any rate, Jesus's prayers going up with ours is the picture here.

To consider the *"Stretch,"* let us remember that Babylon was conquered in one night, while the decline and fall of Rome happened over centuries. The historicist interpretation of the trumpets sees in the first four trumpets the tribes that trampled the infrastructure of the Roman Empire after it moved headquarters to Constantinople. Trumpets five and six are seen to picture the rise of Islamic rule which would have circled the Mediterranean except for being stopped at Constantinople, and stopped on the other end at Tours, Spain, so they could not get to Rome. In the historicist viewpoint, the eating of the little book in Rev 10 signifies the fervor to understand Daniel around 1800, and the adventures of the two witnesses of Rev 11 have to do with the banning of the Bible and God during the French Revolution, 1789–99.

"Now." Since both Revelation and Daniel use this section to show the fall of an empire that neither worships God nor protects people from its own power, perhaps we could look at what happens when greedy organizations, corporations, and governments gain power and make continuation of power their main goal.

For our lessons from the sounding of the trumpets, let us view the trumpets, not as revenge, but as results of oppression, not as arbitrary punishments, but as natural consequences of greed and corruption. Pollution in nature reflects and follows the greedy abuse of nature and people. They are connected. I will suggest directions for Internet research on the losses pictured in the seven trumpets, though there are many additional losses that could yield helpful research.

The sounding of the first trumpet brought fiery destruction to earth. A third of the trees and grass were burned up. In order to make ranches for cattle grazing many of our trees have been burned up. Using the Internet, find out the percentage of forestation lost in the last fifty years. Then get the estimate of the number of species now extinct because of loss of forest habitat. Then research other effects of large-scale deforestation, like drought, and accumulation of greenhouse gases that the forests had previously consumed and transformed into breathable air. Furthermore, it will be interesting to research how many poisons we have put into the soil of our earth to kill weeds or pests, and what happens to all those chemicals.

The sounding of the second trumpet brought a fiery mountain into the sea. A third of the sea creatures and birds died, and ships could not navigate. Using the Internet, discover an estimate of how many species in the sea and sea air have been lost in the last fifty years. Discover the locations of the ocean garbage patches, how they grow and process the trash, and an estimate of how long until ocean life goes extinct from eating the micro plastics and their related toxins. Discover how much of world trade is handled by sea and how the disruption of sea trade would affect what we could buy in our stores.

The sounding of the third trumpet brought a star from heaven to our drinking water. The star was wormwood, a natural substance that causes abortions. The water became bitter, and a third of the population died from the water. Using the Internet, find out how many peoples, or what percentage of people on earth do not have clean drinking water. Discover how many poisons have entered our drinking water sources, either by run-off from the fields or by dumping from our ventures. Consider what kinds of political or economic or social systems would make life very bitter, and what would make abortions popular.

The sounding of the fourth trumpet partially darkened the sun and moon, and took out a third of the stars. Here is a mini preview: In Rev 12 we will see a third of the stars taken down by the dragon who is the devil and Satan. It seems to me that the impairment of earth, seas, water, and stars by one-third capacity is the responsibility of God's enemy, not of God. Using the Internet, discover how many people in the world do not have healthy air to breathe, how many or what percentage of people live in cities with smog warnings in the summers. Research the effect of sunlight on human mental and physical well-being and consider how sunlight has changed over the last fifty years to require the protection of shade and sunscreen.

The sounding of the fifth trumpet brought pests that tortured with their sting and were equipped for battle. They rode under the rule of Destruction and Destroyer. Warfare has changed over the years. Soldiers no longer line up in battle lines and shoot all together in one volley and then another. We learned about guerrilla warfare, where anyone anywhere might shoot at any time. Then we got terrorism, which uses killing with a larger goal to strike terror into people's minds and living. And now we have remote controlled war and war of mind over mind on our own soil. These can be researched on the Internet.

The sounding of the sixth trumpet brought horses that hurt with the fire and smoke from their mouths, and with their tails which also have mouths. This trumpet sounds a lot like continuation of the previous trumpet. In addition, now we know the power of words from the mouth to deceive and intimidate, to blunt the courage of whole nations, let alone that of individuals who do not fit in.

The sixth trumpet has two expansions. Expansion A tells me that those who figuratively eat the Bible, maybe here the book of Daniel, will survive to tell about it again, after finding their belly bitter from the eating. Expansion B tells me that the Bible and belief in even the existence of God may be attacked and apparently killed, exciting a party in the streets, yet the Bible and belief in God will rise again. The witnesses would be those who give testimony for God and Jesus in the Bible and other venues. The clearest message I get from the seven trumpets is that, in order to survive and thrive in what is coming on earth, your and my work in the Bible, in Revelation and Daniel, is very important.

The sounding of the seventh trumpet brought praise in heaven, new views of the temple of God, and more signs in the natural world. I encourage us to take this bit of praise at the end of Rev 11 and make it our own.

In the sounding of the seven trumpets, I believe God has given us a picture of the ills of our world, how they came about, and our best protection, which is connecting with Jesus through reading the Bible and hearing other testimony of him.

Let us summarize quickly here the pointed lessons from the first three sets of seven. From the seven churches we learned to open the door to Jesus. From the seven seals we learned to increase our praying. From the seven trumpets we learned to read the Bible.

SEVEN ANIMALS

For the seven animals and thinking of *"Then,"* I think Christians living in John's day would have recognized immediately the many verbal and image parallels between Dan 7 and Rev 13. Christians with Hebrew background would have smiled at John's skill in repurposing an old story for a new situation. The angel guides in Daniel's visions had identified the empires that fit the first three animals such that the lion was Babylon, the bear was Persia, and the leopard was Greece. I think John's Christians would have had no trouble extending the timeline to see Rome as the dreadful animal. John then took the dragon, in Rev 12, made it red, and made it clearly Rome, seeking to kill Jesus at birth, and then also called it, the "Ancient Serpent," the "Devil," and "Satan." To understand what to expect from the leopard-bear-lion-dragon (LBLD) animal of Rev 13, the sixth animal in our list of seven, all they would have to do is go back to Dan 7 and pick out obvious characteristics of the four empires represented by the animals that were patched together in Rev 13.

Later, Paul can be heard giving an idea of how the Christians might have viewed the empires represented by the four animals. He says the Jews demand signs and the Greeks desire wisdom (1 Cor 1:22–25). I will extend this from my reading to the other empires: Babylon desired glory, Persia desired influence, Greece desired wisdom, and Rome desired worship. It is true, that from this distance, I have just now boiled down whole empires into one word each. It is hardly fair to think that John's first readers would have had one word ready for those empires, being much closer in time to them than I am. However, they would have had a clearer sense in their souls of what drove those empires than I can even imagine. So maybe they would have been looking out for a composite of all the evil traits of all the empires they could remember. They could have noticed that the dreadful animal and the red dragon, and the LBLD animal are all said to have ten horns.

The two-horned animal might have been difficult to understand except that John's Christians could have clearly understood that, at first, he is a counterfeit of Christ, and later, he is a bait-and-switch animal, from lamb to dragon. I believe the prophecy of the animals in Revelation had its parallel in the prophecy of the four animals in Daniel and that the first readers and hearers of Revelation would have recognized and enjoyed the similarities.

For the *"Stretch,"* and to understand the historicist view of these seven animals, all we have to do is look first at Daniel's four kingdoms, Babylon, Persia, Greece, and Rome. Then we let the red dragon stand in for Rome while he shows himself to be inspired by the Devil, waiting as a malevolent midwife to kill Jesus at birth. Being frustrated in this, and seeing the child taken out of his reach, the dragon pursued the mother and all believers in Jesus though they were helped by the earth.

People I know who use the historicist interpretation are quick to explain that the kingdoms Daniel lists were human systems that, in the end, organized themselves against God and the worship of God. Their demise would not be simply the death of the king, or the system organizers, or even all the local people. The judgment is on the system who fulfilled or did not fulfill God's plan for that system.

The next animal, the LBLD animal, lets us see that the drive of Babylon toward glory, of Persia toward influence, and of Greece toward wisdom, all continue in Rome toward being worshiped, while Rome, with its composite influences, continues to the end of the *"Stretch."*

I believe this LBLD animal is usually seen, from the historicist viewpoint, as representing the organization which took over the throne and authority of Rome when the capital moved away to Constantinople. The Roman church did its best to protect the people, provide some infrastructure, and feed the hungry in the gap that the empire left. The two-horned animal is seen as the expansion of the United States under a rule "of the people, by the people, and for the people" as well as a rule of religious freedom and against the intermingling the powers of church and state.

In the case of the seven animals, then, the *"Stretch"* reaches from Daniel's time down to the end of time. I have added the seven animals in an additional column on our timeline. I wish there were a way to show on the timeline how the red dragon is actually behind and through all of them. Instead, I show him as one of the seven. Admittedly, his position on the timeline is somewhat ambiguous.

Seven Animals

Era	Year	Animal
Adam	1000	
Noah	600	
Abraham	500	
Moses	300	
David	0	
Babylon	100	Lion
Persia	300	Bear
Greece	500	Leopard
Rome	700	Dreadful (10)
John	1000	Dragon (10&7)
Constantine	1500	
Pope Gregory I	1800	LBLD (10&7)
Islamic Advancement	2000	
Pope Gregory VII		
Martin Luther		
US Expansion		Two-Horned
Global Advancement		

For the *"Now,"* I will seek to draw lessons for today from the march of the kingdoms through the centuries and the prophecies that highlighted them in either Revelation or Daniel. I believe these seven animals have much to teach about whom we will have, or choose, as king of our lives.

The lion was given human standing on its feet and a human mind (Dan 7:4). King Nebuchadnezzar of Babylon congratulated himself for the great kingdom which he himself had made for his own glory, after Daniel the prophet urged him to stop his oppressions. When I think I did or can do something without God, that is when I start oppressing others in my search for my own glory.

The bear was told to get up and devour many bodies (Dan 7:5). Whenever Persia conquered, or devoured, an area, the empire put forth effort and resources to restore the worship and culture of the diverse people thus acquired. I wonder if, in all my spheres of influence, I am as careful to initiate and protect others' religious freedom as I am my own.

The leopard was given dominion (Dan 7:6). Greek culture spread rapidly and durably everywhere that Alexander the Great advanced. But Paul said the cross of Christ is foolishness to the Greeks, and Christ is the wisdom of God. I want to remember that any time I look for wisdom outside of Christ and the cross, it will fail me.

The dreadful animal had ten horns and teeth like iron. Later it spoke arrogantly against God, persecuted God's people, and presumed to change God's times and laws (Dan 7:7, 25). The court will sit in judgment and his dominion will be taken away. I can take courage in knowing that all arrogance, persecution, and presumption is against God and God will handle it.

The red dragon had ten horns and seven heads (Rev 12:3), noted by "(10 & 7)" on the timeline. He waited to catch Jesus, but Jesus was taken to heaven. The woman who bore him, and later her offspring, became the red dragon's prime targets. They overcame him by the blood of the lamb and by the word of their testimony and by willingness to die if need be (Rev 12:11). These are the ones who keep God's commandments, hear the testimony of others, tell our own testimony, and hold and bear Jesus's testimony (Rev 12:17). The red dragon's story makes me want to keep God's commandments and hold Jesus's testimony.

The LBLD animal also had ten horns and seven heads "(10 & 7)," which were named blasphemously. This animal was like a leopard with feet like a bear and a mouth like a lion. It received its might, headquarters, and authority from the red dragon (Rev 13:1–8). It was therefore a leopard-bear-lion-dragon (LBLD) animal composed of parts of the four who preceded it. It was wounded to death then was healed and came back. Later it spoke blasphemously against God, persecuted God's people, and required worship from all inhabitants of earth. It seems to me that the only way to keep from succumbing to this demand for worship is to have one's name written in the Lamb's book of life. It will require endurance and faith. This animal simply ups the ante in the great war and causes me to pray for endurance and faith.

The two-horned animal was lamb-like only in that it had two horns. It spoke like the red dragon before it and forced worship of the LBLD animal. It used signs and deception. It made an icon or image "(10 & 7?)" of the LBLD animal and then made that icon live. The icon required worship of itself and caused the killing of those who refused (Rev 13:11–15). This looks like the peak of coercion, by fear, shame, guilt, force, and violence. The two-horned animal, speaking like the red dragon, had all the technology necessary to keep track of everyone who refused to worship and to refuse them the necessities of life. No one would be left behind. I get the sense that this animal moved very quickly along the path of war against God. I see no hope, at the end of Rev 13, for those who refuse to worship the icon or its animal, unless we go on to the next chapter and its three angels. I believe God is faithful, and the promises which are buried treasure in the earlier sevens will carry through for this eventuality.

The seven animals show a stark progression in the intensity of aggression toward God and toward God's people. Instructions and promises are sprinkled among the aggressions. Let us join in the research to find them and make them our own.

From the seven animals it is affirmed to me that God sets up and sets aside the kingdoms of this world, and will continue to do so, always.

EXCURSION: THREE ANGELS

Though seven angels are mentioned in Rev 14, there are only two that are numbered. They are numbered "second" and "third." We will follow the pattern and count the one prior to the second as the first of three.

I find threes to be important in Revelation, almost as important as sevens. Did you find the three woes at the end of the seven trumpets? They simply introduce the trumpets that are not part of the first four. There are many more threes in Revelation.[7] Have fun discovering and comparing them sometime! We will examine only the three angels here.

---

7. Here are some more threes in Revelation: Three offers from Jesus (Rev 3:14–22). Three divine persons in the throne room (Rev 4:8–9; 5:6, 13; 4:5). Three cries of "Holy" for the Lord God Almighty (Rev 4:8). Three judgment scenes (Rev 4; Dan 7; Rev 20). Three sections to the old Hebrew sanctuary (Rev 6:9–10; 8:3–4; 11:19). Three woes (Rev 8:13; 9:12; 11:14). Three things the red dragon gave to the LBLD animal (Rev 12:2). Three parts to overcoming the red dragon (Rev 12:11). Three possessions of God's

A person could observe that there are three parts to an X, which is the same shape as the Hebrew alphabetical letter, "chi." There is the top half, there is the bottom half mirroring the top half, and there is the confluence in the middle. If I notice that Revelation is organized like a chi, with a first half, a middle, and a last half mirroring the first half, then this middle is where we are when we approach the three angels. They fly in the fold of prophecy, in what we might call the wrinkle in time. After this chapter the writing makes an orderly progression, coming full circle and closing out every piece that was opened in the first half. However, the time it takes to do this in actual history is stated as being much shorter than in the first half (one hour as compared to forty-two months, for instance). Revelation 14 stands at the jumping-off place, at the entrance to a new kind of action. I believe the structure of the book, this "chiasm," shows us where we are in the prophecy. We have been hanging around in this wrinkle in time until God knows the times are right.

What do we have to comfort us in this wait? What can counter the intense consternation at the end of the story of the seven animals?

Before we dive in for the comfort and guidance, let us step back with a little empathy and consider how the seven animals may be viewing their roles. In Revelation, we have seen some pretty bloody events, wars, and killings, and pestilences. Then in the seven trumpets we have seen all of nature, troubled by pollution and abuse, deteriorate into only two-thirds capacity. The story of the last of the seven animals just might picture a fearful, frantic, gigantic effort to save the planet, to bring all humans into compliance with a plan for global peace and security. Living in the wrinkle may mean that systems get invented and initiated to try in our own power to fix the world against the consequences of our own greed.[8]

---

people (Rev 12:17; 14:12). Three human decrees about worship (Dan 3, 6; Rev 13). Three sixes (Rev 13:18). Three foul spirits (Rev 16:13). Three parts to Babylon at the end (Rev 16:13, 19). Three animals destroyed at last (Rev 20:10).

8. Let us pray for the world leaders making the plans. Here are words from the preamble and para. 3 of 91 of such plans delineated by the United Nations:

> All countries and all stakeholders, acting in collaborative partnership, will implement this plan. We are resolved to free the human race from the tyranny of poverty and want and to heal and secure our planet. We are determined to take the bold and transformative steps which are urgently needed to shift the world onto a sustainable and resilient path. As we embark on this collective journey, we pledge that no one will be left behind....
>
> We resolve, between now and 2030, to end poverty and hunger everywhere; to combat inequalities within and among countries; to build peaceful, just and inclusive societies; to protect human rights and

Let us return now to the three angels and explore the *"Then."* In John's day, any Christians at all familiar with Hebrew culture would know that angels visit humans. They might find the Rev 14 scene unique, however, of angels flying in heaven calling out messages from God.

The first angel, carrying the gospel to all peoples, would have recalled to their minds the promise to Abraham that all families of the earth would be blessed through him and his descendants (Gen 12:1–3). Also, Jesus himself had already indicated they would carry the gospel to all the world (Matt 28:19; Acts 1:8).

Anyone familiar with the Hebrew Scriptures would have recognized and resonated wonderfully with the description of the one to worship as called out by the first angel. "Worship him who made heaven, earth, sea, and springs of water" (Rev 14:7 KJV, WZ paraphrase). This phrasing comes straight from one of the central Ten Commandments (Exod 20:8–11) and is used in Old Testament retellings of creation (Neh 9:6; Ps 146:6), and in New Testament prayer (Acts 4:24). I have noticed that the use of familiar words such as these helps to comfort and inspire.

The second angel, announcing Babylon's fall, brings a scene straight out of the Old Testament story in Daniel as well as from the annals of history. Babylon fell in one night, one hour, as the royalty and bureaucrats were partying and congratulating themselves on how impregnable was their city (Dan 5).

"Stretch." The mega-story, the overarching reach of the historicist interpretation, sees these three angels reflected in spiritual events in the time of United States expansion. Using the historicist interpretation the first angel pictures the time, around 1800, when many around the world were announcing the time of Jesus's coming to judge the world. The second angel pictures the time, beginning a few months later, when there was societal and religious backlash, ridicule, and exclusion of people who preached this way. The third angel pictures a last warning against the animals and the icon, and is still being preached.

"Now." The three angels are quite personal to me. The first angel is the reason I write and preach, and try to reach beyond my cultural comfort zone. I feel it deeply, that the good news must go to all the world, and I want

---

promote gender equality and the empowerment of women and girls; and to ensure the lasting protection of the planet and its natural resources. We resolve also to create conditions for sustainable, inclusive and sustained economic growth, shared prosperity and decent work for all, taking into account different levels of national development and capacities.

(United Nations, "Transforming Our World," Preamble and para. 3.)

to reach especially those who have found the Bible and religion fearful or oppressive. This message is the gospel, the good news, the hope that can live inside humans in the midst of everything ugly.

I find three imperatives in the call of the first angel. One, "Fear God" means, not craven cowering (as in those who do not love God in Rev 6:15–17), but respect and trust (as in those who do love God in Rev 7:14–17). Two, "Give glory to God" means not to give glory to myself (as the king of Babylon did in Dan 4:30), but to give God a high form of praise as used in the heavenly throne room (Rev 4:9, 11; 5:12, 13; 7:12). Three, "Worship him" means no worship belongs to any of the animals or to the icon they make. "Worship him" means not to worship idols made of gold, silver, brass, stone, or wood (Rev 9:20). "Worship him" means a continual bowing down before the Lord (Rev 7:11, 15). Here, then, are three imperatives about whom to respect, give glory, and worship. To me, these imperatives do not appear to be particularly easy, good feeling, or intimately relational. Instead, they appear to be intense, internally motivated, and relationally satisfying in the humans.

The one who is to receive all this respect, glory, and worship is the one who made heaven, earth, the sea, and the springs of water. I find it interesting that these are the four things troubled by the first four trumpets, as if God's creation and even God's authority are attacked by Satan through human inattention to the needs of our world. I find it more interesting that this verbiage clearly recalls the words of the Sabbath commandment, as if God uses that central commandment for purposes of identification for himself. Let us examine it here.

"Remember the Sabbath day, to keep it holy. Six days you will labor and do all your work, but the seventh day is the Sabbath of the Lord your God. In it you will not do any work, you, nor your son, daughter, servant, slave, nor even your cattle, nor the stranger under your hospitality. For in six days, the Lord made the heaven, earth, sea, and all within them, and rested on the seventh day. For this reason, the Lord blessed the Sabbath day, and made it holy" (Exod 20:8–11 KJV, WZ paraphrase). There is his name, "the Lord your God." There is his jurisdiction, "heaven, earth, sea, and everything in them." And there is his authority, "the Lord made them." In one short paragraph and in one weekly day is God's insignia. There is no real puzzle about which day is the seventh since no one questions which day is the first, as in Easter Sunday. Since there are seven days in a week, the seventh day is the one just before Sunday.

If I appropriate for myself this weekly reminder to rest, to stop my own trying to fix my life, and to worship the one who made me, I believe I will be protected from the deceptions of the evil one. God will work his own insignia into my character. The lesson for me from the first angel is that God can fix my life. God can.

The second angel calls out "Babylon is fallen" (Rev 14:8 KJV). This is the first of many mentions of Babylon in the book of Revelation. This one comes shouted from the sky. I remember the tower of Babel was the first effort by humans to save their world, that time from a flood (Gen 11). Their communications broke down and they did not get to finish. Later, the king of Babylon was the one who looked out over his kingdom to cite his "great Babylon, that he had built for his kingdom by the might of his power, and for the honor of his majesty" (Dan 4:30 KJV, WZ paraphrase). His communications broke down, too, and he hardly got to finish his sentence before he was sent on a seven-year sabbatical. The lesson for me from the second angel is that I cannot fix my world. God can. I cannot.

The third angel shouts the final warning. I must decide. There is no more procrastination, no possible fence-sitting. Either I will worship the icon of the animal, or I will worship the God of all creation. I find it interesting that the animal and the icon and the mark are so prominent here in such close proximity to the reminders of the Sabbath commandment. It is as if the mark were the insignia of the evil powers, and somehow a mockery of the insignia of God, while the Sabbath is the insignia of the Lord our God.

If I drank the wine of Babylon that says I can save myself by worshiping the animals and their icon, then I will drink the wine of the wrath of God. This may seem pretty harsh yet it is "because they have shed the blood of saints and prophets" (Rev 16:6 KJV) that they get blood to drink. The lesson for me from the third angel is that my time to decide is now. God can. I cannot. And I decide to let him.

Perhaps as part of this third angel's call stands the next statement of the powers of God's people. Here are those who "keep the commandments of God and the faith of Jesus" (Rev 14:12 KJV) These words call me back to the end of the red dragon's story which highlights those who "keep the commandments of God and have the testimony of Jesus" (Rev 12:17 KJV). There are three things that God's people keep. Someone has said that the reason they can keep the commandments of God is that they do have the faith and the testimony of Jesus. These angelic messages say to me, God can; I cannot; and I decide to let him. May God grant us, by grace, safe keeping of the commandments of God, the testimony of Jesus, and the faith of Jesus.

From reading the three angels I am called to keep the faith and testimony of Jesus, and the commandments. From reading the three angels I am convinced that God can; I cannot; and I decide to let him.

SEVEN PLAGUES

"Then," when the book of Revelation was written, two or three things would have been evident and relevant to the first century readers, about the plagues, or cups, or bowls (Rev 15–16). First, I think they would have noticed the similarity of these first four to the first four of the trumpets encountered a few chapters earlier. The first four plagues land on the earth, the sea, the fresh water, and the sun, this being the same order as for the trumpets. Second, they would have noticed that, in the plagues, the destruction is described as "all," while in the trumpets it is only "one-third." For me, the notation of the destruction of "all" gives this story a sensation of moving much more quickly than was the case with the earlier story.

I think the first-century readers would also have recognized the plagues as striking directly at favorite dependencies of the Roman empire. The sea connected various parts of the Roman Empire for trade and military strength; the Roman aqueducts were famous for bringing fresh water where it was needed; and worship of the sun was becoming popular again beside worship of the emperor. These you can investigate on the Internet.

In the *"Stretch,"* the seven plagues kickstart the world out of the wrinkle in time, the fold of history. It seems to me that their verbal similarities to the trumpets in Rev 8–11, highlight the chapters between them, Rev 12–14, as the central chapters of the book, the U-turn of the writing, the fold of history, the wrinkle in time, the place where humanity has hung out for some time waiting for God to save as many people as possible and whatever else God wants to do to get the stage set for the finale. Once the world flows over that edge the events appear to be more severe and quick.

Let us notice that the red dragon, the LBLD animal, and the two-horned animal show up in the sixth of these plagues, except that the two-horned animal is now called the "false prophet" (Rev 16:13–14). Perhaps the title "false prophet" well describes its bait-and-switch policies (has two horns like a lamb then speaks as a dragon). I see that the role of the three animals here is to gather people together and consolidate the forces for the battle against God.

I also notice that these plagues highlight the various ways in which humans had devastated the earth. If indeed the enforcing of togetherness attempted by the three animals was for the purpose of saving earth's ecology or health, well, it did not work. And now, after leaving the fold of history, all that effort toward coming together to save the earth will apparently be directed toward consolidating against God.

To study the *"Now,"* let us observe the picture, given before the plagues fall, of God's people in a safe place singing the song of Moses and the Lamb,

"Great and marvelous are your works, Lord God Almighty; just and true are your ways, O King of saints" (Rev 15:3 KJV, WZ paraphrase). Moses, the deliverer, and Jesus, the Savior, are named together as authors of this song, and the song seems important for divine protection in the plagues.

The first plague falls against those who worship the icon. This plague is a medical problem, a sore, and it could be global.

The second plague kills every living thing in the sea. From the language used, it seems to me that this might affect only one or several of our oceans or seas.

The third plague turns all fresh water into blood An angel announces that God's decisions are true and fair in that he has given those who shed blood, blood to drink. Let us let God do whatever God finds necessary for truth and fairness.

The fourth plague falls on the sun. Humans are scorched by its heat. By the words of the text, this could be different at different latitudes, or it might be the same around the globe.

The fifth plague falls on the headquarters of the LBLD animal, with darkness so thick and painful in some way that people bite their tongues from pain, yet no one repents to worship God.

The sixth plague releases the powers of coercion and deception that are already in place to gather kings and people together for the great global showdown with God. In light of Jesus's return at a time we do not know, we are to keep our garments, lest we walk naked, and they see our shame. I remember that these garments are bought from Jesus (Rev 3:18) and washed in his blood (Rev 7:14). Without Jesus, his garments, and his blood, I cannot avoid taking on the shame-driven motivations of the society in which we live.

The seventh plague delivers in all-encompassing tones the word, "It is done" (Rev 16:17 KJV). Babylon breaks into three parts, presumably the red dragon, the LBLD animal, and the two-horned animal, here called, the "false prophet." We met Babylon in our last chapter where she was giving out her wine to those who would consort with her. Now she drinks the wine of the fierceness of God's wrath. Please notice, each time God's wrath is mentioned, there is a corresponding statement of human atrocity that makes the judgment true and fair. I believe that in the end of everything, everyone will admit to the truth and fairness on which God's kingdom is built.

Let us also notice that the destruction of the opposing forces happens by their own falling apart, here, breaking into three parts. In Rev 17, it seems that the kings who supported Babylon turn on her to destroy her. For me, the justice is that God finally allows the antagonist to destroy the antagonist's own systems along with the people who stayed with the systems despite the sword-words of truth coming out of Jesus's mouth.

From the seven plagues, I believe we can learn that God's judgments are always true and fair. We can also observe that before and through the plagues, God's people sing the song of Moses and the Lamb, "Great and marvelous are your works, Lord God Almighty; just and true are your ways, O King of saints." Jesus is present in songs which he has empowered them to sing.

SEVEN ANIMALS REVISITED

A while back I admitted that the position of the red dragon on our timeline is somewhat ambiguous. We will now explore some additional complexities connected with the animals and with Babylon. We will be in Rev 17. We will open our keen observations to see many things laid alongside other things, sometimes with a simple "is" or other verb of being. The words "metaphor" and "parable" mean "alongside speech" and, along with several other figures of speech, could be mentioned as a group of "alongside speech." I will let us off the hook of having to decide which "alongside speech" shows itself in each case, whether it be repetition, symbol, metaphor, simile, hyperbole, parable, proverb, riddle, personification, or irony, and let us simply feel the expansion or emotion in the use of this "alongside speech." I believe Jesus's manner of speech can help us understand how "alongside speech" works, whether found in parable, symbol, or simple repetition.

In Matt 24, Jesus *conflates two events,* the destruction of Jerusalem and the end of time. I believe we see that kind of conflation of events in Rev 17, to the effect that a timeline can be only approximate and suggested for Revelation. In John 10, Jesus says he is the shepherd of the sheep and the door to the sheepfold at the same time, for some of us picturing a shepherd who lies down to sleep in the otherwise unprotected gate to the sheep shelter. I believe that kind of *doubling, or tripling or more, of roles* presents itself in Rev 17, such that the LBLD animal may seem to be everywhere, depending on how one interprets him. In Matt 13, Jesus says the kingdom's amazing change from small to huge can be represented by two different things, the mustard seed and the yeast. I believe that kind of overlap of *two or more symbols for one role* may appear in Rev 17, blurring the distinctions between some entities, the woman and the animals, for instance. In Matt 13, the kingdom is the valuable find and, quickly then, the kingdom is the finder of the valuable. I believe that kind of quick *role switch* happens in Rev 17, for instance, where the woman is a whore, is a ruler of kings, and is sitting on waters, mountains, heads of the animal, and the animal itself. These observations caution me that that it would be wise to let my language leave some identities and roles a bit blurry when I talk about them in Rev 17.

I will spend some time stating simply here what can be found in Rev 17, inductively gathering the words of the text that surrounds the symbols and other alongside speech. We will consider "is" and "are" in particular.

Seven Animals Revisited

Figure	Year	Animal
Adam		
Noah	1000	
Abraham, Sodom	700	
Moses, Egypt	600	
David	500	
Hezekiah, Assyria	300	Lion
Babylon	0	Bear
Persia		Leopard
Greece		Dreadful (10)
Rome	100	Dragon (10&7)
John	300	
Constantine	500	
Pope Gregory I	700	LBLD (10&7)
Islamic Advancement	1000	
Pope Gregory VII	1500	
Martin Luther	1800	Two-Horned
US Expansion	2000	Scarlet (10&7)
Global Advancement		

The whore is the woman, is Babylon, is that great city, is ruler over the kings of the earth (Rev 17:5, 18; 14:8; 16:19; 18:10; 18:21). We understood, in our work on the second of the three angels of Rev 14, that Babylon is religion that teaches or exemplifies the worship of self in arrogance against God. For instance, Babel was built to gather and defend the humans against God (Gen 11). Babylon's king claimed to have built all his greatness by himself for his own glory (Dan 4). Another king of Babylon boasted he would exalt his throne and ascend to be like the Most High (Isa 14). We heard from the second angel that Babylon, the religion of "I am god," is fallen, broken, and proven false. Nevertheless, now in Rev 17 we observe that she, Babylon, still rules all kings.

"The waters where the woman sits are peoples, multitudes, nations, and tongues" (Rev 17:15 KJV, WZ paraphrase). The woman, Babylon, sits on multitudes of individuals. She is supported by the people, and perhaps she even treads on people and crushes people.

The woman sits on an animal (Rev 17:3). Let us detour to Dan 7:17 to find that animals are kings, and to all of Dan 7 to learn that the word "kings" here extends to human kingdoms, empires, and systems.

The Scarlet Animal

The animal is scarlet, has seven heads and ten horns, and is full of names of blasphemy (Rev 17:3). It is scarlet, sort of like the red dragon. It has names of blasphemy, sort of like the LBLD animal. It has ten horns like the dreadful animal in Dan 7, like the dragon himself, like the LBLD animal, and supposedly like the icon or image of the LBLD animal, which the two-horned animal made and enlivened. This scarlet animal has seven heads like the red dragon, like the LBLD animal, and like the icon. Thus, to pick the outstanding descriptors to put in one sentence, I say the red dragon and the three animals after him (counting the icon in place of the two-horned animal) have ten horns and seven heads, which become landmark descriptors marking these animals as similar in some way.

It appears to me that the Devil (the red dragon) made three copies of himself. The red dragon made the LBLD animal colorful, a patchwork of other animals, with the landmark ten horns and seven heads, his most durable copy, which later landed in the fire before him (Rev 19:20; 20:10). Next, the red dragon induced the two-horned animal to make the icon of the LBLD animal and give it life, a copy of the copy, supposedly with the landmark ten horns and seven heads. Then, here in Rev 17, we see a third and less durable copy, with the landmark ten horns and seven heads, full of names of blasphemy, ridden by the woman Babylon, and later turning against her to tear her and eat her. It is interesting to me that this train of thought leads to three copies of the dragon in sixth place. Perhaps the red dragon steps in place three times as the sixth animal, maybe hoping never to reach the seventh.

This scarlet animal was, and is not, comes from the abyss, and goes to perdition, attracting wonder from those whose names are not in the book of life (Rev 17:8). Attracting wonder, or worship, from those whose names are not in the book of life gives this scarlet animal a special affinity with the LBLD animal (Rev 13:3, 8). Coming from the abyss gives this scarlet animal an affinity with an animal we have not yet discussed who came up in Rev 11 to kill the two witnesses for God, and then seems to disappear from any further story. I wonder if the later scarlet animal and the short-mentioned animal of Rev 11 could be the same animal, who went more than once to stay in the abyss for a while.

This calls us to try to find out the origination locations for the other animals. In Rev 12–13, the red dragon is said to come from heaven, the LBLD animal from the sea, and the two-horned animal from the land. One could understand these to include the totality of God's creation, heaven, earth, and sea, as involved, at least as interested spectators, in the last things on earth. Or one could compare Rev 17:15 to see the sea as many peoples, earth as not many peoples, and heaven as a superhuman realm.

The scarlet animal arises from the bottomless pit, the abyss. There is a king over the abyss, whose name is Destruction and Destroyer (Rev 9:11). As the place where, later, the devil will be confined for one thousand years, the abyss seems to be the destroyed and devastated earth having no human inhabitant (Rev 20:1, 3; see also Jer 4:23–26). In each of the other Revelation references to the abyss (Rev 9:1, 22; 11:7; 17:8; see also Luke 8:31), the abyss, or bottomless pit, could be read as simply the destroyed and desolate places of the earth, out of which returns an organization, system, or Devil, which had taken a break there.

The seven heads are seven mountains, are seven kings (Rev 17:9–10). Also, animals are kings (Dan 7:17). It seems to me that, putting Daniel's "are" with Revelation's "are," we can conclude that both kings and animals are, by extension, human kingdoms, empires, or systems. I suggest we not be too quick to label any of these merely civil or state powers because, after all, many of them have names of blasphemy.

Of these seven heads, mountains, kings, and animals, five are fallen (as in past) one is (at whatever time the angel interpreter cites) and one is yet to come for a short time (Rev 17:10).

Five are past: Lion, bear, leopard, dreadful animal, and LBLD animal.

One is: Two-horned animal with its icon of the LBLD animal.

One is yet to come: Scarlet animal (perhaps the return form of the LBLD animal).

There are the seven. That is, unless you live in the first century of the Christian era. In that case, you might look for five in the past before either the dreadful animal or the LBLD animal. There will be more on this in a minute.

The animal that was, and is not, is the eighth, is of the seven, and goes to perdition (Rev 17:11). Comparing Rev 17:8, which was considered earlier, we can match the "was and is not" and the "goes to perdition" to know that this is the scarlet animal, who comes from the abyss, and attracts those whose names are not in the book of life. He is the eighth and is of the seven.

For eight, it is lion, bear, leopard, dreadful, dragon, LBLD, two-horned, and scarlet.

For seven, it is lion, bear, leopard, dreadful, LBLD, two-horned, and scarlet.

In Revelation the red dragon is never called an animal, or "beast," as the King James Version translates the word. When there are seven, the dragon sits out as not one of the human kings, empires, or systems. When there are eight there is no term used to label or categorize the constituents of that eight. The text reads "eight" with a slight hiatus waiting for eight "what." There is no "what," and the red dragon sits among the other seven in plain sight the only not-human entity among them. This is why the dragon fits only precariously on my timeline. If this reconciliation of the eight and the seven makes sense, then the scarlet animal is the last of the eight as well as the last of the seven.

There is something else about the eight and the seven which would be good to notice right here. There is an "is not" in the eight and an "is" in the seven. Both the "is" and the "is not" being in the present tense as the angel was telling it, I would expect the "is" and the "is not" to be occurring simultaneously, in different entities, of course.

The ten horns are ten kings (Rev 17:12), human empires, human organizations, or human systems. I observe that the set of ten kings (horns) is different from the set of seven kings (heads, mountains). The seven heads, as kings, seem to operate consecutively over time (five fallen, one is, one yet to come) while the ten horns, as kings, seem to operate contemporaneously (for one hour). There may be a different set of ten for each of the different animals that carries ten horns, the ten horns being human systems that run concurrently with, and support, that animal.

There are ten horns and seven heads on four of the animals and both horns and heads appear to be, here in this penultimate scene, kings, or human empires, organizations, and systems, a set of seven and a set of ten. The ten horns give their empires to the scarlet animal for one hour, the short time mentioned earlier. Then the scarlet animal, with those ten horns, turns against the woman to desolate her and burn her. The scarlet animal appears no more, perhaps subsumed in the LBLD animal's demise, going to perdition.

Then-Stretch-Now

For this section, the *"Then"* will refer to the time when John was being carried away in the spirit and listening to the angel talk, in the first century CE.

We think the early Christians may have called Rome "Babylon" either as a code name or as a deterrent against fraternizing. I think they may have seen Rome both in the whore and in the animals. They would have been familiar with Daniel's list of empires, Babylon, Persia, Greece, and Rome, and known they were in Rome. They probably would have cast about to identify the five in the past before Rome.

Moving around in Revelation, we would discover Sodom and Egypt in Rev 11, Sodom who seduced and oppressed Abraham's family (Gen 19; Ezek 16; 2 Pet 2:8), and Egypt from whom Moses freed the Israelite slaves (Exod 14; Ezek 23). Early Christians could have used Sodom and Egypt to make up the five as shown below. Alternatively, they could have remembered Assyria of Hezekiah's time (2 Kgs 18–19; Ezek 23), though not mentioned in Revelation or Daniel, and used Egypt and Assyria to constitute the five.

Five are past: Sodom, Egypt, Babylon, Persia, and Greece.
Alternative five are past: Egypt, Assyria, Babylon, Persia, and Greece.
One is: Roman Empire.
One is yet to come: Yet to be discovered (Roman Church? United States?).

For them, the future kingdoms were yet to unfold. Let us notice, though, that there was no time during the first or second centuries that Rome was the "is not." If Rome was the "is" then it remains to identify who was the "is not" at the same time.

Readers in the late first century may have known of the legend that Nero would return. Nero was the fifth Caesar-son-of-god emperor of the Roman Empire. The readers after 68 BCE, when Nero died, could have counted five Caesars that had fallen, and pondered the legend, *Nero Redivivus*. One problem with this calculation is that none of us know which Caesar to count as the "is" because they changed quickly after Nero. Another problem with this reading is that the legend died out before very long.

I think that readers during the first and second centuries could have counted heads and animals just as we did and recognized that there was more trouble to come after Rome, or in the permutations of Rome. I also think they believed and hoped it would not take years for this to be accomplished.

For the *"Stretch,"* the way I have described the developments in Rev 17 makes a nice overarching prophecy from early times until the end. We have shown the timeline that follows these animals from about 600 BCE to the end of human kingdoms on earth. They are Babylon, Persia, Greece, Roman Empire, Roman Church, United States, and the return of the Roman Church supporting the conglomerate of all false worship.

However, many people who use the historicist interpretation do not find this satisfactory. They believe the words of the angel in explanation should be understood as spoken to, and taken by, John to refer to his own time, such that the "is" and the "is not" were being accomplished and fulfilled at the time contemporary with John's life in the first century. The question boils down to whether the "is" and the "is not" pertains to John's day or to some time later in the history as marked by prophecy.

I will cite two reasons for letting the "is" and the "is not" stand at a later time than John's day.

One, John states that one of the plague angels initiated this whole conversation, implying that John was, in his vision, securely footed in a time nearer to the last plagues. Further, he states that he was carried away in the spirit to see what he saw, and to hear what the angel explainer told him, as recorded for us in Rev 17. It seems to me that he could have been taken to any time and did not have to stay in his own time. John also states that he was taken to the wilderness, which in Revelation is a place where God's people are protected and nurtured (Rev 12; see also 1 Kgs 19). The prophet would be safe here while watching astonishing transformations among the antagonists to God. For these reasons, I believe that the "is" and the "is not" are at a time in John's future in which both the "is" and the "is not" would be operative at the same time.

Two, Rev 17:9-11 is a riddle, a proverb, a parable, a wisdom saying![9] It can be told in the present tense for whenever it may eventually apply. It seems that one way to solve the riddle would be to find a time in history when one of the eight "is not" while one of the seven "is." It seems to me that the "is not" and the "is" would have to run concurrently since both appear with "is," backed by the same Greek word. I view the LBLD animal, wounded to death, as the "is not," and the two-horned animal, with his icon of the LBLD animal, as the "is." Many who use the historicist interpretation see this "is not" and "is" time starting around the end of the eighteenth century, with the capture and imprisonment of the head of the Roman Church (is not) and with the rise of the United States (is).

Regarding the roles of the Roman Church, it seems to me that most people who use the historicist interpretation do not seem to halt at the Roman Church being cast in two or more roles, as fatally wounded in 1798, as astonishingly revived, and as both carrying and partially composing the conglomerate of all false worship, labeled Babylon. For people who use the historicist interpretation, this fits in the mega-story, the overarching narrative. The narrative is a war story that begins before the earth was created and

---

9. For instance, think of these pieces of "alongside speech" spoken in the present tense: (1) "What goes up and doesn't come down?" (2) "What is black and white and red (read) all over?" (3) "Three men walk into a room . . ." (4) "Wisdom cries in the streets" (Prov 1:20 KJV, WZ paraphrase). (5) "A man, having found treasure hidden in a field, hides it again in the field, goes and sells all that he has, and buys the field" (Matt 13:44 KJV, WZ paraphrase).

ends when all evil has confederated against God and burned itself out in the last battle. Earth has become new again.

"*Now*," for a quick review and warning, let us notice some identifying marks of the primary antagonists in both Revelation and Daniel. Their identifying marks appear to include (1) speaking blasphemy, great words against God (Dan 7:8, 20, 25; 8:23; 11:36; Rev 13:5–6, 8), (2) attempting to change God's law (Dan 7:25; Rev 12:17), (3) warring against God's people (Dan 7:21, 25; 8:24; Rev 12:17), (4) using force and killing (Dan 11:38; Rev 13:15; 17:6; 18:24), (5) using deceit and flattery (Dan 11:23, 32, 34; Rev 12:9; 13:14; 18:23; 19:20; 20:3, 8, 10), (6) controlling wealth (Dan 8:25; 11:43; Rev 13:17; 18:3, 11–18), and (7) maintaining power for 1260 years at one sitting (Dan 7:25; 12:7; Rev 11:9, 11–12; 12:14; 13:5). It seems to me that God surely wants those who understand to recognize the Devil's work (Dan 11:33, 35; Matt 24:15; Rev 13:18).

I do know that the end is worth it. The ultimate scene is worth all the puzzle and riddle, all the mouth and all the war against God and God's people. The ultimate scene is where I will be grateful to have been kept on God's side. This future, entered into by imagination during inductive reading of Revelation, affects for the better all my current choices. Truly, *the happiest book I ever read is the Revelation of Jesus Christ.*

SEVEN LAMENTS[10]

A lament is a loud grief, loud in decibels and loud in internal pain, and sometimes called a wail. We will now examine seven laments or wails that were made about Babylon Rev 17–18.

"*Then*," when John wrote, the story of Babylon was an empowering story for Jews, a community-building story for the Jews. Jews had been captive in Babylon, the poor ones especially oppressed and longing for home in Jerusalem. Then Babylon fell in one night to the Medes and Persians. The new kings sent the Jews home with their own temple treasures, which had been kept in foreign treasure rooms and used in ridiculing God and Israel.

At the time of the writing of Revelation, "Babylon" may have been a code name for Rome. Rome was oppressing the poor and the Christians, while making trade and pleasure the highest values. The laments correctly positioned what was happening in the Roman empire at the time John wrote.

---

10. My research on the organizational systems comments on the seven laments included Cook with Baldwin, *Love, Acceptance and Forgiveness*; Friedman, *Failure of Nerve*; Richard, *Apocalypse*; Rowland, *Radical Christianity*; Tonstad, *Revelation*.

For the *"Stretch,"* people who read with the historicist method of interpretation see that Babylon was split into three parts and assume that these three parts would be the three entities of Rev 12–13, the red dragon, the LBLD animal, and the two-horned animal, otherwise called the "false prophet." To me, it seems plausible that the text pictures Babylon as made up of these three organizations as a world super-system.

Coming near the end of the overarching narrative, Babylon is a system, as were the animals, not the individual persons who work and live within the system. The individual persons have their place in the picture as, together with other individuals, making up the waters on which the woman Babylon sits. This looks to me like the woman uses the people, is propped up by the people, and treads on the people (Rev 17:15).

Also, the words that are common and parallel between the laments and the seals confirm for me the chiastic nature of the whole writing and the existence of this fold of history, or wrinkle in time, depicted at the center of the book of Revelation. Thinking in terms of the long-reaching interpretation, the world is catapulted out of that slow-moving fold of history at the falling of the seven plagues. Here activity accelerates. Big things happen in one hour or one day (Rev 18:8, 10, 17, 19; 17:10, 12), much shorter time than the forty-two months, the five months, or even the three and one-half days cited in the pages before the center of the book. I see the world going over the cliff into lightning-speed action in gargantuan events.

Since we who use the historicist method of interpretation consider ourselves to be living still in that fold of history, before the hurricane of activity, perhaps we could take notice and make some preparation. I suggest the best preparation is to spend time with the living Christ in this book that wants to reveal him to us.

"Now," these laments are like the curses or woes after the blessings in Deut 28, Ps 1, and Luke 6. In the next section we will discover the seven blessings; here we study the seven laments. I believe it might do us well to begin lamenting now, to let some of our prayers be confessions of our world's marginalizing of God, and to notice where our choices fit those of the fallen systems around us. Lament is appropriate for a Christian to do. Lament brings the situation into words and lays it out before God. Lament recognizes the problems without blaming, or rushing to fix them, apart from God.

In the seals we saw organizations built up, organizations that had dreams of producing highest good and worked through obstacles to realize those dreams. In these laments I find that, in the end, organizations fail people. The only system created by God and not humans is the family, and yes, many times the family fails its people because of its human element. I have noticed that systems created by humans fail their people sooner or later for the very reason that they are human and leave room for human arrogance and corruption to rise to the top. And we lament, we wail, we mourn.

Though it may be sad, let us explore what it is this woman Babylon shares. It is called the "wine of the wrath of her fornication" (Rev 14:8; 17:2; 18:3 KJV) on which she herself is drunk. Fornication, in a spiritual sense, would be going after and getting in bed with other gods, other than the God of creation and the Bible (as did Jerusalem, Sodom, and Samaria in Ezek 16, Ahola and Aholibah in Ezek 23, and Gomer in Hos 1–3). It seems we humans hope to meet our human needs our way, by hooking up with any number of false promises, like sex, drugs, overwork, drunkenness, diverse doctrines, and Satan worship. None of these can give us anything but fear, shame, and guilt which, I suggest, is in the cup which the woman gives to all who cavort with her and which, I suggest, is false doctrine about the character of God.

Core and Tools of Deception and Coercion

I remember that the deception and coercion of the antagonist in Revelation, whether animal or woman, first showed itself in the placing of stumbling blocks (Rev 2:14) and seductions (Rev 2:20) in the way of God's people. Deceit came into the open in Rev 13:14 but had earlier forms in claiming to be something one is not in the first, third, fourth, sixth, and seventh churches (Rev 2:2, 9, 20; 3:9, 17). Finally, the deception and coercion added onto its stumbling blocks, seductions, and deceits, the killing of those who resist (Rev 6:11; 11:7; 13:7, 15). I see the deception and coercion growing throughout Revelation from the core of stumbling blocks, seductions, deceits, and killings, using the tools of fear, shame, and guilt.

The fornication of the antagonist is first begun in the context of the stumbling block and seduction happening in the third and fourth churches (Rev 2:14; 20–23). In today's world sexual liaison is one of the surest ways of producing long-lasting fear, shame, and guilt. By guilt I mean something like obligation, or the vulnerability to having a "guilt trip" laid on. I have observed that, whether or not children result from the sexual liaison, this kind of liaison creates a channel for the passing or sharing of guilt and obligation, as well as of fear and shame.

Fear is not allowed in the new heaven and new earth (Rev 21:8). Yet, many of today's systems speak fear, either by focus on the increasing ills in our world, or by veiled threats of what the large organization can do to the little human. It is for this reason, I believe, that we live with simmering fear in more people now than ever before.

Shame is mentioned twice in Revelation, both times connected to the state of nakedness produced either by not having bought clothing from Jesus (Rev 3:18), or by not keeping that clothing ready at hand for any contingency (Rev 16:15). The clothing is white (Rev 3:18; 6:11; 19:8, 14), washed and made white in the blood of the lamb (Rev 7:14), and defined as the righteousness of God's people (Rev 19:8).

The problem for me is that I know that in myself is no stable or inherent righteousness at all, and in answer to that problem I see that it is the blood of Jesus that makes the garments white, by forgiving my sins and cleansing me from all unrighteousness (1 John 1:7–9). This is good news for me. I can live clothed in forgiveness which banishes shame. When the evil one shames me for my many shortfalls, I can, at that moment, confess that shortfall, wash my clothes in the blood of Jesus, and stand without that shame. This, I believe, is the good news of the Revelation of Jesus Christ, *the happiest book I ever read.*

This is what I see in Scripture: obligation, or the vulnerability to a "guilt trip," is all over the three animals at the end of the seven of which we read in Rev 12–13. The red dragon gives the LBLD animal his power, place, and authoritarian prestige. For this reason, the LBLD animal is obligated to the red dragon and does not seem to mind putting obligation onto the world to worship the red dragon. The two-horned animal obligates himself by making something like the LBLD animal, an icon to which he gives life. Obligation, or fear, shame, and guilt, is what ties these three together. Fear, shame, and guilt are the tools of the antagonist in Revelation, and the wine of which the woman makes all nations drink.

This is what I see in our world: fear, shame, and guilt are contagious and get passed around among intimates and down along generations. Fear, shame, and guilt, used as motivation or control, spread the contagion. If a system could be purged of fear, shame, and guilt, there would still be the child who had it beaten into him before the purge and would inevitably bring it back. In systems built by fear, shame, and guilt, there is systemic anxiety and no room for collaboration, empathy, or creativity. Freedom only makes room for the most cunning exploiter of fear, shame, and guilt to take over the rule of the system. People who imbibe the fear, shame, and guilt soon produce it for themselves, and one day have enough fear, shame, and guilt that they want no other for a leader than one who rules by fear, shame, and guilt.

In Revelation it seems clear to me that this Babylon who rules the world and makes everyone drink of the wine of the wrath of her fornication does not rule by love as Jesus does. She rules by fear, shame, and guilt and gives it to the people to drink. Now, before the destruction of this system, God calls us into love, acceptance, and forgiveness, the realities of God's character, for the eradication of all of Babylon's wine even within us.

Yes, I will carry the fear, shame, and guilt spread upon me by Babylon's wine unless I let Jesus in. He says to the last church, Laodicea, "I love you, and I will rebuke and reshape you if you will only let me in. I'm knocking" (Rev 3:19–20 KJV, WZ paraphrase). He says to the first church, Ephesus, "I was your first love, and you have left me. Repent, return, revive your first love" (Rev 2:4 KJV, WZ paraphrase). Then the fear can have no hold on you (1 John 4:18).

Everyone who knows Jesus is saying, "Come; whoever will may come and freely drink the living water" (Rev 22:17 KJV, WZ paraphrase). This call extends perfect acceptance with Jesus. If I can read this book of the Revelation of Jesus Christ and fill my inner being with that divine acceptance, then I can live in a bubble of acceptance for myself and accepting others exactly where they are. There, shame will be conquered.

We have already visited the blood of the Lamb as the magnificent clothes-whitener. The blood of the Lamb is the abundant forgiveness that is available to us through Jesus's death (1 John 1:7–9). I can walk about my life in the glorious forgiveness of Jesus that makes my clothes whiter than mere washing-machine white. I can walk about freely forgiving others and, in the process, freeing myself from any guilt and obligation connected to those liaisons. The forgiveness of God is powerful. The author of Revelation announces that God's people overcame the red dragon by the blood of the Lamb and by the word of their testimony (Rev 12:11). I find no guilt and no possibility of obligation in the forgiveness of Jesus. The blood of Jesus overcomes guilt.

In Jesus's new reign, love, acceptance, and forgiveness[11] will have pushed out fear, shame, and guilt, and I believe these can never rise again.

In Rev 17, all the organizations of the world agreed to unite and give their fear-shame-and-guilt power to one organization, so they would have aggregate power to fight against Jesus, the Lamb. The union did not last long, and various organizations began to hate the big one and to tear her apart (Rev 17:12–14). Fear, shame, and guilt as controllers in society give way to oppression, violence, and drunkenness, and cannot hold the massive machine together. This is the destruction that comes upon the whole Babylon system. I understand that this is how the living Jesus overcomes, while initiating no violence.

---

11. Cook with Baldwin, *Love, Acceptance and Forgiveness*.

If we can hear the laments before the fall of Babylon and take the precautions prescribed, may the Lord have mercy to bring us into living by love, acceptance, and forgiveness. Let us now hear and join the laments.

Return to Laments

For hope to help us endure through long lament let us let our minds be drawn away to a picture that is happening at the same time as the dramas with the animals and the laments over Babylon. A white horse strides out of heaven whose rider is called "Faithful and True" and "The Word of God." He has many crowns and a sharp sword of words from his mouth, and he conquers in the last great battle of earth. Then he calls us to his wedding. Oh, follow the story in your inductive reading. For me, the very reading of it inspires joy and hope and the strength to endure.

Now let us review the seven laments of Rev 18 to get acquainted with the city Jesus builds out of love, acceptance, and forgiveness.

The first lament repeats the announcement that Babylon is fallen and mentions nations and kings and merchants as those who have drunk of Babylon's wine. It is written that the king of Babylon says, "Is not this great Babylon, that I have built for the house of the kingdom by the might of my power, and for the honour of my majesty?" (Dan 4:30, KJV). Perhaps we could lament today that nations as well as their kings and merchants, so often buy into the system's presuppositions that production is everything and consumption must support production, so we live in a society bent on saving itself by purchasing and producing. I believe fear, shame, and guilt shout, "Just try harder! Always try harder." Jesus invites us into play.[12] Play under the protection of his love, acceptance, and forgiveness.

The second lament calls God's people to come out of Babylon lest they partake of her sins or her plagues. Her claim sounds much like that of the king of Babylon, "I sit a queen, and am no widow, and shall see no sorrow" (Rev 18:7 KJV). Maybe we could lament today that the system glorifies itself and lives luxuriously while not giving much thought to the poor or the environment. I find that the fear-shame-and-guilt message is "Go along to get along." Even the poor go along hoping to get along better. Jesus calls us out! Jesus invites us to differentiate ourselves, come out of that system into a very different kind of rule, that of love, acceptance, and forgiveness.

The third lament is by the kings of the earth who have lived deliciously with her, as they bewail her while keeping their distance now. Perhaps we

---

12. For the invitations from Jesus in my lessons from the seven laments, I am informed by Friedman, *Failure of Nerve*.

could lament how the primacy of production and consumption feeds the build-up of other industries like finance and marketing and transportation. I have observed fear, shame, and guilt piling information on information, ever more quickly storing it and retrieving it and gathering more. Jesus invites us to decide for him today, no matter what information we do not have yet, and live in love, acceptance, and forgiveness.

The fourth lament is by the merchants of the earth who have been made rich by trade in this production-and-consumption-dependent system. They lament that no one buys their merchandise anymore and the richest luxuries cannot be found anymore. Most distressing is the listing of slaves and the souls of humans as some of the products traded in this system. Let us lament for the slaves and human souls that are being sold in sex trade, tortured, extorted, and made to endure other abuses today. I believe the fear, shame, and guilt in retail creates an anxiety to gain certainty about trends and rates and transportation and laws. Maybe we even carry over that craving for certainty into our thoughts about God. Instead, Jesus invites us into adventure under the rule of his love, acceptance, and forgiveness.

The fifth lament is by the sea traders, sailors, and captains, and all in sea industries. They bemoan the fact that Babylon made all ship owners rich by her demands and now she is gone. Let us lament our dependence on demand and lament the lies in our marketing to create unhealthy and exaggerated demand in this system. I observe that fear, shame, and guilt drove our marketing cadre to capture quick and unexamined human reactions and then use them to tell the lie that everyone is doing it. Now Jesus says, "Choose for yourself." We can freely choose under Jesus's rule of love, acceptance, and forgiveness.

The sixth lament is by an angel who takes up a huge stone and throws it into the sea, saying this is what will happen to Babylon. The angel says the greatest people of the earth were deceived by this system's lies and seductions, and this system is responsible for the deaths of prophets, and God's people, and all who were slain on the earth. We might lament the greatest people lost, the most inhumane motives and actions condoned and encouraged, and the deaths of good people. I find that fear, shame, and guilt drive the system and its people to discover blame and find scapegoats. Instead, Jesus invites us to support and encourage each other's strengths and to find ways to engage and better-up their projects, always with love, acceptance, and forgiveness.

The seventh lament drops over into Rev 19 (you remember the chapter divisions are a relatively new phenomenon) and is said by a great voice of many people in heaven. Perhaps we would like to learn to say what they say, "Alleluia; Salvation, and glory, and honor, and power, be unto the Lord our

God, for true and righteous are his judgments" (Rev 19:1–2 KJV). He has avenged the blood of his servants which cried out to him in Rev 6:11. They were told to wait a little while, and indeed, it did not take long once it began. Let us notice and lament the time they waited, which must have seemed interminably long. I think it is fear, guilt, and shame that produces urgency in any work or process. Jesus invites us to trust to him the time it will take as well as the finishing of the process under love, acceptance, and forgiveness.

Laments and mourning and grief are usually considered sad. Instead, it is the fear, shame, and guilt that are sad. Under Jesus's rule of love, acceptance, and forgiveness, we can play and differentiate, decide and adventure, choose, and support both strengths and process. Though the system will try to bring us back in, we can carry with us a circle where others want to be, in love, acceptance, and forgiveness. And finally, Jesus will ride forth on a white horse, the conqueror, having let all who held onto the fear, shame, and guilt fight against each other, tear each other apart, and eat up one another.

From reading the seven laments in Revelation, I understand that lamenting is helpful and encouraging sometimes, when we keep the Lord our God, the living Jesus Christ in view, as revealed in this book, the Revelation of Jesus Christ.

SEVEN BLESSINGS

We will not find a section of Revelation labeled "Seven Blessings." Yet there are seven blessings scattered among the other material. By way of concluding this section of this book, we will adventure out to find and gather the blessings. The word behind our word "blessing" connotes happiness, wealth, health, and honor.

At times throughout the preceding chapters, we have noticed that the animals represent kingdoms, empires, organizations, or systems, and not individual persons. Most of them also dabble in the business of worship, so these are empires wherein religious and civil laws are at least somewhat intertwined. Only one is a bit different, the two-horned animal does not even talk about worship until he has made and enlivened the icon to be worshiped. I wonder if maybe he got a glimpse of restraint about government not establishing religion, and later renounced that insight.

I affirm the common historicist disclaimer that the prophecies mostly deal with organizations or systems, even churches, and not individual persons. On the other hand, on this current adventure we will finally pull together the gems scattered among the systems, that are written for the individuals in these systems. Humans look for freedom, find creativity, and eventually experience death, as individuals. When individuality flourishes, then empathy, listening, and collaboration can happen to help us get through the global difficulties. Let us cherish the seven blessings.

For the *"Then,"* I perceive that the first-century readers would have been familiar with blessings. Moses set up the form, even having the blessings called from a mountaintop, and curses from another mountaintop (Deut 28:1–68; 30:1, 19; Josh 8:34). David carried it on in the first psalm, showing blessing for some and not blessing for others. Jesus used the form effectively in his inaugural sermons, at one point making them blessings and woes. (Matt 5; Luke 6). When this book of the Revelation of the living Jesus Christ opened with a blessing, it would have been no surprise or puzzle.

For the *"Stretch,"* the scattering of these blessings throughout the writing makes me think the seven blessings may be trans-century in effect, ready to be claimed as promised blessing at any time during the overarching mega-story and meta-narrative. However, for further study, it seems that noting the blessings' placements in the book of Revelation and their immediate contexts might bring us added insights.

For the *"Now,"* let us examine each of the seven blessings to find lessons for today.

The first blessing is, "Blessed is the one who reads, and those who hear the words of this prophecy, and keep those things which are written therein: for the time is at hand" (Rev 1:3 KJV, WZ paraphrase).

I have always believed that there is a mighty blessing for those who read or hear this book, whether or not they think they understand it all, or at all. This is the reason I have read Revelation over and over countless times. This is why I go about encouraging simple inductive reading of Revelation, as the Revelation of the living Jesus Christ. The promise of this blessing is given at the very beginning of the book so I will see it almost first when trying to read or memorize.

The second blessing is, "Blessed are the dead who die in the Lord from here on: Yes, says the Spirit, they may rest from their labors; and their works do follow them" (Rev 14:13 KJV, WZ paraphrase).

We have nothing to fear, and expect only blessing, from death. This promise of blessing appears in the central section of the book, in the fold of history, when the animals appear and develop and three angels fly with messages from God that amount to "God can, I cannot, and I decide to let him." Let us not limit this blessing in death to those who die during the time of the three angels. Since no one will be able to prove this by experiment, I am happy to let the earlier readers enjoy the blessing, too, and to take it up for myself.

The third blessing is, "Blessed is the one who watches, and keeps his or her garments, so as not to walk naked, in visible shame" (Rev 16:15 KJV, WZ paraphrase).

This promised blessing is attached to the announcement of the sixth plague. The world has worshiped the animal, the plagues are the result of such rejection of all good. The sixth plague calls the world to account for itself in battle at Armageddon. Then, dropped there in the middle of the action, without attribution, the words say, "Look, I am coming as a thief. Blessed is the one who watches and keeps his or her garments" (Rev 16:15 KJV, WZ paraphrase). I will not know at what moment, so I had best keep watching now, because apparently the garments are important.

These garments would be those purchased from the living Christ to cover human nakedness (Rev 3:18), or those given to them (Rev 6:11), or those washed and made white in the blood of the lamb (Rev 7:14). It is important to be on watch to keep our garments because Jesus is coming soon and at a time not expected.

The fourth blessing is, "Blessed are those who are called to the marriage supper of the Lamb" (Rev 19:9 KJV, WZ paraphrase).

In the last part of Revelation there may be some conflation of images going on. This is one instance. I may get called to the marriage supper as a guest only to find that I am actually the bride along with all other believers. And I will be dressed in fine white linen, which is here defined as the righteousness of the saints (Rev 19:8). I will assure you that it is not my own rightness and fairness that entitles me to wear white. These white garments have been purchased from the living Christ, given to me, and washed in the blood of the Lamb. And I am blessed now to be called, whether individually or as part of the bride of the living Jesus Christ.

The fifth blessing is, "Blessed and holy is the one who has part in the first resurrection. On this one the second death has no power. They will be priests of God and of Christ and will reign with him a thousand years" (Rev 20:6 KJV, WZ paraphrase).

This blessing is promised in the midst of Revelation's final disposition of the dragon, that old serpent, the devil, and Satan. The reason death holds no fear for God's people is that they will be raised in the first resurrection, to see the finish of everything. Daniel makes a similar claim of two resurrections. "Many of those who sleep in the dust of the earth will awake, some to everlasting life, and some to shame and everlasting contempt" (Dan 12:2 KJV, WZ paraphrase). I read this as a long sleep and then resurrection to see the Lord totally conquer the devil who has so long troubled people. The one who comes up in the first resurrection, cannot die again, but will be among the kings and priests to God (Rev 1:5–6).

The sixth blessing is, "Blessed is the one who keeps the sayings of the prophecy of this book" (Rev 22:7 KJV, WZ paraphrase).

This matches the blessing in Rev 1:3 to make a double blessing, thereby sure and imminent, for those who read the book of the Revelation of the living Jesus Christ. This blessing is set in the context of Jesus's soon coming. "Behold I come quickly," he said, "blessed is the one who keeps the sayings of the prophecy of this book" (Rev 22:7 KJV, WZ paraphrase).

I am blessed by simply reading and picturing the things mentioned as surrounding Jesus's coming. There is a new heaven and earth with no more advancing, encroaching sea. God will be close, and we will all be youthful with no more death, sorrow, crying, or pain. There is a river of flowing water from which I can drink as I drank of mountain streams in the wild when I was young. There is a tree with glowing diverse fruit and leaves that heal all people. There is the throne of God and no more curses. There the light comes from God, and they need no fuels that burden the air. God's people will rule all with love, forever. Everything is new.

I will be blessed to see the healing of the earth, not by human organizations or systems, but by God himself. I suggest, by what I read in Rev 22, that earth must be very important to God.

I have been intrigued by the promise of no more sea. I think the sea now means, for humans, distance, danger, displacement, and destruction, and at that time all those sadnesses will be no more. Furthermore, the sea was the origination place for many of the ominous animals in Revelation and Daniel. There will be no more sea. God will reclaim and restore the earth. I am blessed by Jesus's coming quickly.

The seventh blessing is, "Blessed are those who do his commandments. They will have right to the tree of life and to enter through the gates into the city" (Rev 22:14 KJV, WZ paraphrase).

Apparently, doing his commandments is still the basis of citizenship in that new country where the living Jesus reigns. This blessing recalls to my mind the double description of God's people at the end of time in the fold of history. Twice it is said that they keep the commandments of God (Rev 12:17; 14:12). In these statements, keeping the commandments is clearly connected with having the testimony of Jesus, on the one hand, and the faith of Jesus, on the other hand. The kind of faith Jesus had while on earth would enable the keeping of the commandments. The testimony of Jesus, which Jesus gave while on earth and which is given by believers, is also important for keeping the commandments.

Twice identified in Revelation, and then once blessed, as commandment keepers, we could believe that keeping the commandments of God is important for God's people. I want us to review the Ten Commandments for a minute to help us understand the nefarious nature and bad behavior of the opposition to God in the book of Revelation.

Exod 20:1–3 proclaims God as the only God and no one able to take his place, but blasphemy, which is putting a person in place of God, is rampant among Revelation's antagonists (Rev 2:9; 13:1, 5, 6; 16:9, 11, 21; 17:3).

Exod 20:4–6 inveighs against idols, but the antagonists of Jesus in Revelation both practice and teach idolatry (Rev 2:14, 20; 9:20; 21:8).

Exod 20:7 protests using God's name falsely, but at least one of the animals in Revelation is described as the one who was, is not, and yet is, a play on God's name (Rev 17:8, 11; compare Rev 1:4, 8; 2:8; 4:8).

Exod 20:8–11 is a reminder to keep the Sabbath as a sign of the Creator God. In Revelation, humans worship demons, idols, the LBLD animal, and the icon rather than the God who created all things, and they do not worship on the day that is the commemoration of creation (Rev 9:20; 13:4, 8, 12, 13; 14:9, 11; cf. Rev 4:11; 14:7).

Exod 20:12 insists on honor to those who went before, but in Revelation shame instead of honor gets thrown about as one of the animals torments and kills the witnesses and refuses them burial while the people celebrate their deaths (Rev 11:7–10). Perhaps the most shameful is the willingness to put stumbling blocks and seductions in the way of fellow humans (Rev 2:14, 20). Satan as the red dragon is the most prolific producer of shame as he accuses our siblings day and night (Rev 12:10).

Exod 20:13 weighs in against murder, but murder permeates the stories of Revelation (Rev 6:11; 9:21; 11:7; 13:15; 21:8; 22:15).

Exod 20:14 declaims against adultery and fornication, and in Revelation fornication is most troubling because of the controlling and God-forgetting ties it produces and the fear, shame, and guilt it spreads (Rev 2:14, 20, 21; 9:21; 14:8; 17:2, 4; 18:3, 9; 19:2).

Exod 20:15 protests stealing. In Revelation theft is mentioned only once (Rev 9:21), yet, in addition, war against people is an effective means by which thefts on a gargantuan scale can be accomplished, and war against God's people is common in Revelation (Rev 11:7; 12:7, 17; 13:4–5, 7; 17:14; 19:19).

Exod 20:16 inveighs against lies, but lies, seductions, and deceptions are the trademark operational manner of Revelation's antagonists (Rev 2:2, 9, 20; 3:9; 12:9; 13:14; 20:3, 8; 21:8, 27; 22:15). After all, it is as a "false prophet" that one of them masquerades (Rev 2:20; 16:13; 19:20; 20:10).

Exod 20:17 proclaims against coveting, that is, cultivating even hidden desires that are unlawful. In Revelation it is the dragon, the ancient serpent, the devil who covets. He wants the baby Jesus, and he wants the woman (Rev 12:4–5, 13–17).

All these bad behaviors help to move the Revelation story forward toward their final natural consequence, death by the word-sword-truth that comes out of the mouth of Jesus.

The lessons for today in the seven blessings are myriad. I think I would be blessed if I were to read them over and over again and even memorize them. One thing is sure, that my salvation and entrance into the beautiful afterlife is not of my own accomplishment but by my staying connected to Jesus. Further, I have found that one of the best ways to stay connected to Jesus is by reading and rereading again the Revelation of Jesus Christ.

CONCLUSION TO LESSONS FROM THE SEVENS

It is time now for the big summary of all the sevens. Before we finish, let us look ahead. There is much more to learn from Revelation and its companion book, Daniel.[13] Let your imagination draw you deeper and deeper in, even about the things that you have read in this little book.

What Were the Lessons?

In this book, we examined lessons from the seven churches as tips from Jesus on how to communicate and get along in small church groups.

Then we observed lessons from the seven seals on how organizations and projects get initiated, grown, and left behind, yet also how to turn around the demise in that life cycle if we will.

We received lessons from the seven trumpets that help us understand how nature sickens under the hand of organizations and corporations that will not turn back.

We spent some time in the central section, the fold of history, where seven animals come from heaven, sea, and earth, and three angels fly in the

---

13. Here are only a few suggestions of the many that could be made for further reading and curiosity, to follow and compare: the temple-tabernacle scenes, the throne scenes, the judgment scenes, the books, the sets of worship words scattered throughout the book, the sets of three, the sets of four, the sets of twelve, the sixth stages, the fifth stages, the material between the sets of seven, other sets of seven not listed as series, the war of the mouths (sword, word, testimony, witness, hurt, blasphemy), the significance of Sodom and Egypt (Rev 11:8) as compared to the other kingdoms, the use and changes of tenses (especially in Rev 13 and 17), the places of origination for each of the animals, the demise of each of the animals, the two women and the Lamb, the connections to Daniel, and wherever it is stated that something "is" something else or these "are" those other things.

sky to bring God's messages to earth dwellers. The angels' messages are God can, I cannot, and I decide to let him.

Next, we observed as the seven plagues completed the work of the trumpets, totally breaking the back of all nature and breaking apart human empires and organizations.

Then we watched the seven laments complete the seals by mourning the demise of the organizations and systems of earth and giving us a heads-up set of tools for thriving now despite systems who deal in fear, shame, and guilt.

Finally, we studied the seven blessings, scattered about through the book, as they completed the promise to the churches in God's organization.

Revelation's structure completes each front part on its way out the back end from the center. The mere reading of the book of Revelation in order yields a feeling of closure, of coming full circle, of completion.

Where Was Jesus?

Further, we heard the living Jesus as he dictated instructions to the seven churches on how to be a calming presence with others.

We saw the living Jesus as the only one able to open up the ways that organizations work, to unseal the pictures necessary for organizations to grow.

We saw the living Jesus praying with the prayers of all his people as nature begins to trumpet its traumas.

In the centerfold of the book, we saw Jesus born as a baby on our earth, into cosmic danger, and then ascending to heaven. We watched the dramas of seven animals and three angels and noticed the three things that God's people have and keep, the commandments of God, the testimony of Jesus, and the faith of Jesus.

Before the plagues could fall, we found Jesus's people singing the song of Moses and the Lamb, the living Jesus.

While people are lamenting the fall of all human organizations no matter how magnificent, Jesus is seen riding out on a white horse to gather all his people.

Riding on the white horse, Jesus calls his people to his wedding feast and blesses them with his loving presence forevermore.

We have read the Revelation of Jesus Christ, *the happiest book I ever read!*

3

Invitations to Discussion

INTRODUCTION: GROUP HOMEWORK AND DISCUSSION GUIDE

What follows is a set of simple aids to curiosity in reading, along with some discussion prompts.[1]

It is my bright hope that you can gather with a few of your friends who can and do commit to

- read Revelation,
- practice play, adventure, curiosity, and imagination,
- meet to listen to each other,
- take turns and respect each other,
- enjoy silence,
- curb talk-over and crosstalk so that quiet people can talk, and each person can feel fully heard.

By this means, I hope we can let Jesus heal us and our world from fear, shame, and guilt as motivation and control, and instead cultivate in us and in our world love, acceptance, and forgiveness. This is why, for me, the book of Revelation is *the happiest book I ever read.*

1. My research for these discussion guides included Doukhan, *Secrets of Daniel*; Doukhan, *Secrets of Revelation*.

INVITATIONS TO DISCUSSION 87

To make this a daily devotional project to last a year, use each guide sheet for three days, dividing the questions 1–2, then 3–4, then 5, or another way if it works best for you. This will give you devotional work for 366 days.

Perhaps you would like to keep a growing record of the praise words you encounter, paraphrase them for yourself, and use them in individual worship or together as a team.

May your group fellowship be sweet.

REV 1:1–3

1. Apocalypse. Where have you heard the word? What did it mean in that setting?
2. Read or listen to Rev 1:1. List the persons involved in the origin, transmission, and reception of this piece of prophecy. Discuss the possible identity and role of each.
3. Read or listen to Rev 1:2. Discover other instances in Revelation of the words "word of God." Read their contexts. Ponder and discuss the meaning and consequences of the word of God (Rev 1:2, 9; 6:9; 19:13; 20:4).
4. Read or listen to Rev 1:2. Discover other instances in Revelation of the words "testimony of Jesus." Read their contexts. Ponder and discuss the meaning and consequences of the testimony of Jesus (Rev 1:2, 9; 12:17; 19:10).
5. Read or listen to Rev 1:3. Discover other instances in Revelation of the word "blessed" used at the beginning of a pronouncement. Read their contexts. Ponder and discuss (Rev 14:13; 16:15; 19:9; 20:6; 22:7, 14).

Prayer Prompt: What means the most to you out of today's reading of Rev 1:1–3? What will you do about it today?

REV 1:4–6

1. Do you remember your elementary school learning of the parts of a letter? Tell someone else if you can name them.
2. Read or listen to Rev 1:4–5. Who wrote this letter? To whom? Who sent the greeting of "Grace and peace"? Discuss the possible identity and role of each.

3. Read or listen to Rev 1:5. What are the three descriptors used of Jesus? Discover another instance in Revelation of the words "faithful witness" (Rev 3:14). Read and discuss its context.

4. Read or listen to Rev 1:5. Ponder and discuss the meaning of the phrases "first-begotten of the dead" (Rev 1:18; 2:8) and "prince of the kings of the earth" (Rev 6:15).

5. Read or listen to Rev 1:5-6. Picture in your imagination the three things Jesus has done for us, "loved us," "washed us" (Rev 7:14), and "made us kings and priests" (Rev 5:10). Which matters most to you? Read 1 John 4:10-11, 19. What difference does it make that Jesus "loved us"?

Prayer Prompt: What means the most to you out of today's reading of Rev 1:4-6? What will you do about it today?

REV 1:7

1. When did you first hear of Jesus coming back? What are your feelings whenever you hear or think about his return?

2. Read or listen to Rev 1:7 and Rev 22:7, 12, 20. Who is the one coming in each case? With what does he come? What else does he bring with him?

3. Read or listen to Rev 1:7, also Rev 6:15-17; 20:11-12. Describe the most prominent feelings of people who see his return. What do you think are the causes?

4. Read or listen to Rev 1:7 and Matt 24:30. Ponder and discuss: What does it mean and how could it be that "every eye will see him"? Even those who crucified him?

5. Read or listen to Rev 1:7; 14:14, 19; and Matt 13:30. Please notice, there is no story anywhere in the Bible showing a second-chance time after Jesus gathers his believers. Spend a little time and thought imagining yourself as one of the people Jesus will gather to be with him at the time of his coming. Describe your picture to your group.

Prayer Prompt: What means the most to you out of today's reading of Rev 1:7? What will you do about it today?

REV 1:8

1. Tell about a time you heard or participated in a performance of Handel's "Messiah." Describe your feelings about great art.
2. Read or listen to Rev 1:8, also Rev 21:6; 22:13. Discover two other phrases that explain or define "the Alpha and the Omega." Find one of those phrases in Rev 1:17 and in Rev 2:8 and discover to whom they refer.
3. Read or listen to Rev 1:8, also Rev 1:4; 4:8. Who is the one who "was, and is, and is to come"?
4. Read or listen to Rev 1:8, also Rev 4:8; 11:17; 15:3; 16:7, 14; 19:6, 15; 21:22. Who is the Almighty? What does the name mean? Compare Hos 12:5 and Amos 9:5, and discuss.
5. Read or listen to Rev 1:8. Then scan or read all of Rev 1 and Dan 1, and also Ruth and Esther. What would you say is the theme that shines in all of these? How is that theme reflected in Rev 1:8? How is that theme represented in your life?

Prayer Prompt: What means the most to you out of today's reading of Rev 1:8? What will you do about it today?

REV 1:9-11

1. Tell someone who will listen well about a time you were startled by a sound. Was the sound loud or soft? Near or far? Other?
2. Read or listen to Rev 1:9, also Rev 1:2; 6:9. Discover the two things for which God's people might be imprisoned or killed. Discuss what these two things might mean by reading and comparing Rev 19:10-13.
3. Read or listen to Rev 1:10. Describe the place, the day, and the sound John experienced. Compare Exod 20:10; Lev 23:3; and Deut 5:14 to discover John's likely meaning in mentioning "the Lord's day."
4. Read or listen to Rev 1:10, with Isa 13:9; Ezek 30:3; Joel 2:1-11; Amos 5:18-20; and Zeph 1:14-16. Do you think there might be a second meaning in the mention of "the Lord's day" in John 20:19?
5. Read or listen to Rev 1:11. Do you recognize the name of any of the cities of the seven churches? Put the name of your city in the list and describe how you feel being included.

Prayer Prompt: What means the most to you out of today's reading of Rev 1:9–11? What will you do about it today?

REV 1:12–18

1. Play this game quickly: What is the first word that comes to mind when you hear the name . . . Jesus? Tell someone.
2. Read or listen to Rev 1:12–18. Which piece of this description of Jesus means the most to you today? Why?
3. Read or listen to the other sightings of Jesus in Rev 5:6; 19:11–16. Compare and contrast. Discuss. Tell which piece is most meaningful to you from all the pictures given of Jesus.
4. Read or listen to other sightings of Jesus after his resurrection in Luke 24:13–53; John 20:19–31; 21:1–25; and Acts 1:1–14. To which characters in these stories do you most relate?
5. Read or listen again to Rev 1:12–18. Notice John's feelings as he saw Jesus this way. Please give to each other the gift of listening as you explore the feelings of seeing Jesus.

Prayer Prompt: What means the most to you out of today's reading of Rev 1:12–18? What will you do about it today?

REV 1:19–20

1. Do you remember any of your "Story About My Summer" essays you wrote as a child in school? Tell about the experience.
2. Read or listen to Rev 1:19–20. Look at the context, the chapters on either side of this excerpt, and discover whether or why you think this a good conclusion of one piece and introduction of another.
3. Read or listen to Rev 1:19. Compare Dan 2:28, 45. What two kinds of things was John told to write? What two time frames might we expect to read about in Revelation?
4. Read or listen to Rev 1:19; and Dan 2:28, 45. Compare Gen 41:25, 32. What is God's reason for giving two or more pictures or prophecies of the same thing?

5. Read or listen to Rev 1:20. Find where these items are first mentioned in Rev 1. Start a list of symbols of which the Bible itself tells the meaning.

Prayer Prompt: What means the most to you out of today's reading of Rev 1:19–20? What will you do about it today?

REV 2:1–7

1. Use a digital device to find one fact about the present or past city of Ephesus. Tell someone who will listen.
2. Read Rev 2:1–7. Notice the commendation and the condemnation for the church in Ephesus. Do you think the two parts might be related?
3. Read Acts 19:18–20. Scan the nearby context to this passage. What were some of the beginnings of this small church in Ephesus?
4. Read Eph 4:2, 15, 25–32. Reflect on how the little church pictured in Acts 19 could have come to the place of needing the exhortation given by Paul in Eph 4.
5. Read Rev 2:7. Compare Rev 22:1–2, 14; and Gen 2:9; 3:22–24. Describe some images that come into your mind as you think about the Tree of Life. Do you see yourself there near it?

Prayer Prompt: What means the most to you out of today's reading of Rev 2:1–7? What will you do about it today?

REV 2:8–11

1. Use a digital device to discover one fact about the present or past city of Smyrna (now Izmir). Tell someone who will listen.
2. Read or listen to Rev 2:8–11. List some good things about the church in Smyrna. Describe the trouble in Rev 2:9. Compare Rev 3:9 to gain and discuss a clearer picture of "blasphemy" and "synagogue of Satan."
3. Read or listen to Rev 2:10. List the two commands or imperatives found here for effectively dealing with the trouble mentioned earlier. In your opinion, will these help when someone is talking ignorantly and harmfully?
4. "Smyrna" means "myrrh." Read Matt 2:11; Mark 15:23; and John 19:39. In reflecting on the three times Jesus was given myrrh while on earth,

decide and discuss what might "myrrh" have to do with the letter to Smyrna or to others?

5. Read or listen to Rev 2:11. What images come into your mind as you think about the Crown of Life?

Prayer Prompt: What means the most to you out of today's reading of Rev 2:8–11? What will you do about it now?

REV 2:12–17

1. Use a digital device to discover one fact about the city or church in the city of Pergamos/Pergamum. From where did the idea and word, "parchment," come? Tell someone who will listen.

2. Read or listen to Rev 2:12–17. List some good things about the church in Pergamos, otherwise called Pergamum.

3. Read or listen to Num 24–25. Summarize the story of Balaam and Balak from Numbers and compare this to its retelling in Rev 2:14–15. Both names, "Balaam" and "Nicolaitans," mean "to conquer the people." How might these names be appropriate?

4. Read or listen again to Rev 2:12, 16. With whom will Jesus fight? Using what weapon? Compare Heb 4:12.

5. Read or listen to Rev 2:17. If you could choose a new name right now, what might it be? And what would it mean to you? Would you tell anyone or would you keep it secret? Please take a moment now to picture Jesus giving you a new name.

Prayer Prompt: What means the most to you out of today's reading of Rev 2:12–17? What will you do about it now?

REV 2:18–29

1. Use a digital device to discover one fact about the city or church in the city of Thyatira. Check Acts 16:14 for a couple more facts about Thyatira. Check Rev 2:19 for some descriptions of good in Thyatira. Tell someone who will listen.

2. Read or listen to Rev 2:18–29. Compare the letters to Pergamos and Thyatira, noticing the same sins (sex and food around idolatry), and

the use of OT metaphors (Balaam and Jezebel). Which letter has the longer message? Which has a call to repent?

3. Read or listen to 1 Kgs 16:30–21:29; 2 Kgs 9:30–37. What do you think of first when you hear Jezebel's name? What do you think is the reason her story is mentioned in Revelation?

4. Read or listen to Rev 2:24–25. What are the instructions for believers in Thyatira and the compassion in those instructions?

5. Read or listen to Rev 2:26–28. Who will rule? Who will be broken? When are they broken, before the rule or during or after the rule? What or who is the morning star to you?

Prayer Prompt: What means the most to you out of today's reading of Rev 2:18–29? What will you do about it now?

REV 3:1–6

1. Use a digital device to discover one fact about the city or church in the city of Sardis. Tell someone who will listen.

2. Read or listen to Rev 3:1–6. What kind of reputation (name) did Sardis have?

3. Read or listen to Matt 23:13–33. What possible similarities do you see between the Pharisees and Sardis?

4. Read or listen to Rev 3:2–3. Find five things the church in Sardis was told to do. If they did not watch, what would happen? In this case, what will be the thief's advantage? Discuss what these five imperatives might mean in your life now.

5. Read or listen to Rev 3:5. Compare Acts 3:19. Name two things that can be blotted out. Which would you rather have blotted out? What feelings might you experience when Jesus confesses your name in front of the Father and the angels?

Prayer Prompt: What means the most to you out of today's reading of Rev 3:1–6? What will you do about it now?

REV 3:7-13

1. Use a digital device to discover one fact about the city or church in the city of Philadelphia. Tell someone who will listen.
2. Read or listen to Rev 3:7-13. How much strength did the church in Philadelphia have? With what results? What two things had these believers done well?
3. Read or listen to Rev 3:9-11. Discover and discuss three promises to the church in Philadelphia, besides the "overcomers" promise. What one thing were the believers to do?
4. Read or listen to Rev 3:7-11. Find hints of what the enemies of this church were up to. Compare, contrast, and discuss the stories in Matt 4:5-11 and Luke 4:9-13 with believers' experiences in Philadelphia.
5. Read or listen to Rev 3:12. If you had lived through the kind of opposition that the church in Philadelphia had, what would it mean to have God's name written on your person?

Prayer Prompt: What means the most to you out of today's reading of Rev 3:7-13? What will you do about it now?

REV 3:14-22

1. Use a digital device to discover one fact about the city or church in the city of Laodicea. Tell someone who will listen.
2. Read or listen to Rev 3:14-22. Discuss and compare the two things Jesus said these believers were: middling, lukewarm, so-so (Rev 3:15) and extremely wrong and unfortunate (Rev 3:17). How can both descriptions be true?
3. Read or listen to Deut 8:11-9:6. From where comes the power to get gold and righteousness and eye salve?
4. Read or listen again to Rev 3:14-22. Discover and discuss some phrases or images of hope for Laodicea.
5. Read or listen to Rev 3:20-21. Describe your meal with Jesus. Who all is present? What does his knock sound like? How do you feel when he makes eye contact with you? What does he tell you while you eat? What do you tell him? Compare all this with what eating with Jesus might be like in the great banquet after he comes again (Rev 19:6-9).

Prayer Prompt: What means the most to you out of today's reading of Rev 3:14–22? What will you do about it now?

REV 4:1–2

1. Tell someone who will listen well about the last movie you watched. Did someone invite you? Where did you watch it?
2. Read or listen to Rev 4:1–2. Scan all of Rev 4 to immerse yourself in the context. What would you say is the theme of this chapter?
3. Read or listen again to Rev 4:1–2. Compare Rev 3:7. Where are the doors open in your life right now? How do you feel about a door open in heaven?
4. Read or listen again to Rev 4:1–2. What invitation is offered? By whom? To whom? What did it sound like?
5. Read or listen again to Rev 4:1–2. What was John's immediate response to the invitation he heard? What is your response to Jesus's invitation today?

Prayer Prompt: What means the most to you out of today's reading of Rev 4:1–2. What will you do about it now?

REV 4:2–8

1. Did you ever want an answer, but your teacher or mentor insisted you learn something else first? Tell someone about it.
2. Read or listen to Rev 4:2–8. If you were to entitle this section, what would you call it? What was John shown before he could be shown the future?
3. Read or listen again to Rev 4:3–6. Take a few moments to ponder, imagine, and immerse yourself in the sights, sounds, and fragrances of this throne scene. Then try to describe it to someone else.
4. Read or listen again to Rev 4:2–7. Research and consider seven Spirits of God (Isa 11:2–3), twenty-four elders (Matt 27:51–53), and four creatures with various heads (Ezek 1:4–14; 10:8–22). Discuss what you think they mean here.

5. Read or listen again to Rev 4:8. What did the four creatures continually say? (Compare Rev 1:8; 11:17; 15:3; 16:7; 21:22.) What is your most continual response to God?

Prayer Prompt: What means the most to you out of today's reading of Rev 4:2–8. What will you do about it now?

REV 4:8–11

1. Tell someone who will listen well about something you made that gives or gave you great pleasure.
2. Read or listen to Rev 4:8–11. This includes the first and second of a trilogy of praise in this section of Revelation. Can you find the other in Rev 5? In what ways do they grow?
3. Read or listen again to Rev 4:9–10. Name at least two things they did to show their worship. What physical things do you do to show your worship? What else could you do?
4. Read or listen again to Rev 4:11. Discuss the meaning of the words, "created all things." Review the biblical account of this creation in Gen 1–2. Can you hold in your mind as true both this picture of creation and the discoveries of science?
5. Read or listen again to Rev 4:11. Describe the meaning for you of the word "worthy." Discuss how it feels to be made and held for the pleasure of God.

Prayer Prompt: What means the most to you out of today's reading of Rev 4:8–11. What will you do about it now?

REV 5:1–4

1. Tell someone who will listen well which was your favorite book at ages ten to twelve, and which is your favorite book now.
2. Read or listen to Rev 5:1–4. Where was the book? What did it look like? What was wanted with the book? Ponder and discuss the presenting physical aspects of this scene.
3. Read or listen to Dan 12:4, 9. What was Daniel told to do with his book? Compare Rev 22:10 for what John was told to do with his book.

Discuss what you think might be some connections between Daniel and Revelation.

4. Read or listen to Rev 20:12 and Rev 3:5. Compare Dan 7:9, 10. In these instances what happened upon the opening of the books? How many different books are there? Are they pages or scroll? Or could they be electronic?

5. Read or listen again to Rev 5:1–4. Describe some mystery about this book. What questions are raised by this passage? What questions and emotions did John have?

Prayer Prompt: What means the most to you out of today's reading of Rev 5:1–4. What will you do about it now?

REV 5:5–7

1. Tell someone who will listen well about other names you have been called and how you felt about them.

2. Read or listen to Rev 5:5–7. List at least three names for Jesus found in this passage. How do you know it is Jesus? Discuss what these names might mean as metaphors.

3. Scan Rev 5 to settle into the context. Discuss any evidences you can find as to the importance of the book in view here.

4. Read or listen again to Rev 5:5–7. Describe and discuss how you picture this book with its seven seals. Specifically, does each seal open a part of the book and when all seven are opened you have seen the whole book? Or must all seven seals be broken before you can see any of the book?

5. Read or listen again to Rev 5:5–7. Discuss what is it about Jesus that would give him authority to deal fully with something that deeply concerns humans. Write and share a piece of praise for John to say on seeing Jesus take the book.

Prayer Prompt: What means the most to you out of today's reading of Rev 5:5–7? What will you do about it now?

REV 5:8-14

1. Have you ever been somewhere that felt big and grand and awe-inspiring? Talk about it with someone who will listen.
2. Read or listen to Rev 5:8-14. Pick out all the words of praise to God and pray them back to him today. Find an environment in which to pray that matches the tone of these words for you. Tell someone about your experience in this.
3. Read or listen to Rev 5:8 and compare Rev 8:3-4. What happens to the prayers of the saints in each instance? Discuss what are the similarities between prayers and incense?
4. Read Rev 1:12-13; 6:9; 5:8; 8:3. List and describe the pieces of worship furniture you find mentioned in these verses. Tell how familiar you are with the Old Testament tent of meeting, or sanctuary, and its worship around this furniture.
5. Read or listen again to Rev 5:8-14. Pray again, and again, and always again. Would you commit with me this week to pray praise to the God of Revelation and do it often?

Prayer Prompt: What means the most to you out of today's reading of Rev 5:8-14? What will you do about it now?

REV 6:1-2

1. Tell someone who will listen well about a project you started with great expectation, excitement, and gusto.
2. Read or listen to Rev 6:1-2. Scan and review all that went before this in Revelation. Who is the Lamb? What are the seals he opens? What is it they keep closed? Where are these four creatures? Compare what they said at different times.
3. Read or listen to Rev 6:1. The word "apocalypse" means opening or bringing out of secret and is properly translated "revelation." Discuss how this verse continues this theme.
4. Read Rev 6:2 and compare Rev 19:11-14. Some want to make the four horses into bad and fierce judgments from God. Imagine some other interpretations, always looking for Jesus because this is the Revelation of Jesus Christ.

INVITATIONS TO DISCUSSION 99

5. Read or listen again to Rev 6:1–2. You have been given the things you need to conquer in life, a bow and a crown. What are you doing with them?

Prayer Prompt: What means the most to you out of today's reading of Rev 6:1–2? What will you do about it now?

REV 6:3–4

1. Tell someone who will listen what the Bible has meant to you in some project you undertook. If you did not know about the Bible at that time, try to imagine and share what it could have meant to that project.
2. Read or listen to Rev 6:3–4. This is second in a series of four. What are the colors of the four?
3. Read or listen to Rev 6:3. Compare John 1:45–46. Who has said "Come and see" to you? Who opened your understanding to something new? Have you thanked that person?
4. Read Rev 6:4 and compare Matt 10:34–39 and John 14:27. When you started a new project with joy, what were some things that gave you trouble? Tell someone what you did about these.
5. Read or listen again to Rev 6:3–4. You have been given a great sword, the Bible (see Eph 6:17; Heb 4:12). How are you using it? What kind of weapon is it in your hands, offensive or defensive? Are you letting the Bible and the Spirit cut away your own offenses?

Prayer Prompt: What means the most to you out of today's reading of Rev 6:3–4? What will you do about it now?

REV 6:5–6

1. Tell someone who will listen well about the spoken or unspoken rules of an organization or group to which you belong. Discover and tell some history on one of those rules.
2. Read or listen to Rev 6:5–6. Which seal is broken? Which creature says, "Come and see"? Look back in Rev 4:7 to describe a picture of this creature.

3. Read or listen to Rev 6:5. What color was this horse? What colors preceded this one? What does the rider have in his hand? Do you think he rides out threateningly or hopefully?

4. Read or listen to Rev 6:6. From where does the voice come that sets up the rules of commerce? Of which could a poor person buy more, wheat or barley? The price is a day's wages; the measure is how much a worker can eat in a day. How fair are these prices?

5. Read or listen again to Rev 6:5–6. Why do you think oil and wine are mentioned as protected? What might hurt them? Is this proclamation to limit the famine? Protect the rich? Preserve healing potions? What have you intentionally protected and preserved for your life, family, or group?

Prayer Prompt: What means the most to you out of today's reading of Rev 6:5–6? What will you do about it now?

REV 6:7–8

1. Think of an instance in which longstanding rules turned out to be unfair to someone. Discuss the possible causes.

2. Read or listen to Rev 6:7–8. Scan Rev 4–6 to remind yourself about the seals, the creatures, the person opening the seals, and the horses that came before this one.

3. Read or listen to Rev 6:8. What color was this horse? Think "looking sickly." When leaders in a project, business, or church start worrying more about their own survival than about their mission, what are some strategies or plans they invest?

4. Read or listen to Rev 6:8. Who rides this horse? Think pests, pollution, resistant illnesses, epidemics, and a lack of calling on God. Research and describe the life cycles of some projects, businesses, or churches that are larger than local.

5. Read or listen again to Rev 6:1–8. Review the four stages in the life cycle of a project, organization, or church. Tell of instances in which you have seen these stages. Discuss possible ideas for changing the normal cycles at some point.

Prayer Prompt: What means the most to you out of today's reading of Rev 6:7–8? What will you do about it now?

REV 6:9-11

1. Do you know anyone whose career was killed because of layoffs by a company trying to survive? Describe.
2. Read or listen to Rev 6:9-11. Compare Gen 4:10 and the surrounding story. What does victim blood cry out from the ground? Compare Ps 13 and discuss.
3. Read or listen to Rev 6:11. What was given to them? For the white robes, compare Rev 19:8. Then scan Rev 7 to discover and discuss more talk of white robes and what the context indicates they might mean.
4. Read or listen to Rev 6:11. For the rest that was promised them, compare Rev 14:13. Tell about a recent funeral you attended. Describe what it would be like for you if you could view death as sleep and rest.
5. Read or listen again to Rev 6:1-11. Review the four stages in the life cycle of a project, organization, or church. From this fifth seal or stage, what can you think would be needed for a dying project to be revitalized?

Prayer Prompt: What means the most to you out of today's reading of Rev 6:9-11? What will you do about it now?

REV 6:12-17

1. Describe a situation in which attempts to solve a dispute broke down because of lack of respectful listening.
2. Read or listen to Rev 6:12-17. List and describe the pieces of this picture. Let the images into your imagination just as they come from the words. Describe the feelings they evoke.
3. Read or listen to Rev 6:12-14. Name some calamities, or natural consequences, that come on businesses, organizations, projects, or families that fail to listen to those they have excluded, or to those whom their policies have hurt.
4. Read or listen to Rev 6:15-17. Besides natural consequences, every nation, church, and family, every organization of people, will face the Creator God in the end. What is the question of top interest and urgency?

5. Read or listen again to Rev 6:12–17. Compare and contrast Ps 24. Notice differences and similarities in the tone and outcomes of the readings and whether you read it for one person or for institutions and groups. What will be your prayer today?

Prayer Prompt: What means the most to you out of today's reading of Rev 6:12–17? What will you do about it now?

REV 7:1–2

1. Discuss with someone who listens well the feelings that accompany the global increase in wars over the last twenty years.

2. Read or listen to Rev 7:1–2. Describe and discuss what significance you find in the close ties this scene has with the question "Who will be able to stand?" of Rev 6:17.

3. Read or listen to Rev 7:1–2. Read, compare, and discuss other Bible contexts for the mention of "four winds"—Jer 49:36; Ezek 37:9; Dan 7:2; 8:8; 11:4; Zech 2:6, Matt 24:31; Mark 13:27.

4. Read or listen to Rev 7:1–2. Compare the four angels of Rev 7:1 with the one angel of Rev 7:2 by direction, stance, or movement, and what they hold. Discuss what might be the significance of a seal of God appearing during the opening of seven seals on a book?

5. Read or listen again to Rev 7:1–2. Read also and compare Matt 24:6–8. Ponder and discuss how global wars and the rumors of them can be only the beginning of troubles, as Jesus said.

Prayer Prompt: What means the most to you out of today's reading of Rev 7:1–2? What will you do about it now?

REV 7:3

1. Have you ever felt protected during some present or potential disaster? Tell about it with someone who will listen.

2. Read or listen to Rev 7:3. Describe the backstory from Rev 7:1–2. Why do you think the earth, sea, and trees are protected? Compare Rev 8:7–8; 9:4; 12:16; 13:1; 21:1.

3. Read or listen to Rev 7:3. Ponder and discuss what it would mean for humans to be sealed by God. Claimed, owned? Secret, hidden? Protected from tampering? Never disloyal ever again? Compare Rev 5–6; 9:4. For further, deeper study, compare Isa 8:16–20.

4. Read or listen to Rev 7:3. Ponder and discuss what it would mean to be servants of God, and when and where they serve him. Compare Rev 7:15; 22:3–4.

5. Read or listen again to Rev 7:3. Ponder and discuss the forehead. What makeup or mark goes there? What part of the mind lies behind it? Compare Rev 13:16; 14:1; 22:3–4. For further, deeper study, compare Isa 45:22, and consider in which direction you want your forehead to be looking.

Prayer Prompt: What means the most to you out of today's reading of Rev 7:3? What will you do about it now?

REV 7:4–9

1. When someone excludes me, I can grow bigger and include them. Do you agree? Discuss.

2. Read or listen to Rev 7:4–9. Name, compare, and contrast the two groups cited here. Consider size, ethnicity, and importance of group, whom they serve, and what they receive.

3. Read or listen to Rev 7:5–8. Scan and compare this with the other Bible lists of the twelve sons/tribes of Israel (Gen 49; Num 1–3; 26). How is the order different? Who is missing? Who is included?

4. Read or listen to Rev 7:4–8. Consider the significance of the numbers. Four, the number of earth (Rev 7:1) mixed with three, the number of God (Rev 1:4–5), yields the product of twelve, the number of God's kingdom on earth (twelve patriarchs, twelve apostles). "Thousand" may be a mistranslation or merely a marker of augmentation or intensity. (On the other hand, compare Rev 21:16–17.)

5. Read or listen to Gen 12:1–3. Notice that God would bless Abraham and his seed so they would be a blessing to all nations. Discuss the promise circles drawn in the sand around Abraham. Who is included? Who is secondarily included? Who is excluded? Compare Gal 3:7–9, 14, 29.

Prayer Prompt: What means the most to you out of today's reading of Rev 7:4–9? What will you do about it now?

REV 7:9–14

1. Tell someone who will listen well what you usually do when facing someone whose name you feel you should know but do not.
2. Read or listen to Rev 7:9–14. Who gets the glory and praise in this reading? How many times? In how many ways? For how many reasons? Discuss together.
3. Read or listen to Rev 7:9–14. To consider the meaning of the white robes, compare Rev 6:11 and 19:8. To learn what the palms in their hands might signify, compare John 12:13.
4. Read or listen to Rev 7:10–12. Describe the worship pictured here, what they do and what they say, and to whom. What other words might we use today for this?
5. Read or listen again to Rev 7:9–14. How do you feel about the proximity of great tribulation and great praise? About washing in blood and coming out white? About having nothing to present to God other than what God has given you?

Prayer Prompt: What means the most to you out of today's reading of Rev 7:9–14? What will you do about it now?

REV 7:14–17

1. Describe in detail to someone who will listen your picture of paradise, the best place and events of which you can possibly think.
2. Read or listen to Rev 7:14–17. Structurally, this is the end of the interlude between the sixth and seventh opening of seals. The end of most six-to-seven interludes in Revelation is a preview of paradisal endings. Where are these people? What are they doing?
3. Read or listen to Rev 7:14–17. Compare and contrast other sightings of paradise (Rev 21:1–5; 22:1–5; Isa 11:5–9; 65:17–25). Let yourself imagine and share.
4. Read or listen to Rev 7:16–17. Why do you think hunger, thirst, sun-heat, and tears are especially mentioned?

5. Read or listen again to Rev 7:17. The Greek word for what the Lamb does is "shepherd" them. Compare Ps 23 and Rev 22:17. Compare also Rev 2:27; 12:5; 19:15, because the Greek word translated "rule" means "shepherd." Discuss.

Prayer Prompt: What means the most to you out of today's reading of Rev 7:14–17? What will you do about it now?

REV 8:1

1. Do you enjoy silence? What would it take to get you some silence? What would it take to get you to like it? Discuss this with friends you trust and respect.

2. Read or listen to Rev 8:1. Compare and contrast the noise at the opening of the sixth seal (Rev 6:12–17) with this silence at the opening of the seventh seal. Consider location, characters, observers, etc. Discuss the value of silence.

3. Read or listen to Rev 8:1 with Num 14:34 and Ezek 4:4–6. The only time conversion scale given in the Bible is one day equals one year. Regarding Rev 8:1, one-half hour would be one forty-eighth of a day which, in converted time, equals one forty-eighth of a year. By doing the math, explain this and discuss: One-half hour of silence in heaven in prophetic time could represent how much time on earth in real time?

4. Read or listen to Rev 8:1. Read Gen 1 for seven first days of silence as only God's voice was heard creating. Look ahead to Rev 8:7–8, 10, 12 to notice how some created things on earth will be affected after this moment of silence.

5. Read or listen again to Rev 8:1. Review the opening of each of the seven seals in Rev 6–7 and discuss how a moment of silence could effectively conclude these events.

Prayer Prompt: What means the most to you out of today's reading of Rev 8:1? What will you do about it now?

REV 8:2-5

1. Tell your group several settings where one can hear trumpets played and what emotions each setting raises in you.
2. Read or listen to Rev 8:2-5. Read Num 10:8-10 to discover and discuss two things trumpets primarily meant in Hebrew and Jewish settings.
3. Read or listen to Rev 8:2-5. List the words or phrases that have to do with worship or rituals of worship, either anciently or currently. Compare Rev 5:8 to learn what the incense represents. What feelings does it produce in you to read here that the angel threw the censer of incense and coals of fire to the earth?
4. Read or listen to Rev 8:2-5. How does this reading refer back to and conclude the previous chapters about the seven seals? Compare Rev 6:9-10. Looking at the seals as life-cycle stages of a dream, project, company, church, or institution, where are Rev 8:2-5 in the life cycle?
5. Read or listen again to Rev 8:2-5. How does this reading bridge to, and introduce, the following chapters about the seven trumpets? Compare Rev 11:15-19. Looking at the seals as the life cycle of a dream, project, company, church, or institution, do you think the trumpets will be doom or revitalization?

Prayer Prompt: What means the most to you out of today's reading of Rev 8:2-5? What will you do about it now?

REV 8:6-7

1. When people say Revelation is full of violence from a vengeful God, they find evidence in Rev 8-9. Discuss together what you think and feel about violence attributed to God.
2. Read or listen to Rev 8:6-7. If the seven seals (Rev 6:1—8:5) show the life cycle of enterprises, in particular the faring of the church down through the ages, and if the throwing down of the censer (Rev 8:2-5) shows the ending of something, then the seven trumpets could show the steps in the demise of an enterprise. Discuss.
3. Read or listen to Rev 8:6-7. Research the demolition of trees and other green life on our planet. Discover and discuss locations, causes, and effects.

INVITATIONS TO DISCUSSION   107

4. Read or listen to Rev 8:6–7. There are three things I want us to remember as we explore the seven trumpets. The first is that the censer thrown to earth (Rev 8:2–5) also shows a new and great connection between heaven and earth and that prayers continue to arise effectively during the sounding of the trumpets.

5. Read or listen again to Rev 8:6–7. Glance ahead at Rev 9:4, 20–21 to discover and discuss two additional things besides prayer that might protect an individual during the time of the demise of surrounding corporations, churches, and projects.

Prayer Prompt: What means the most to you out of today's reading of Rev 8:6–7? What will you do about it now?

REV 8:8–9

1. In your experience and opinion, what is the difference between a) revenge, b) punishment, and c) natural consequences? Discuss the three terms with someone you trust.

2. Read or listen to Rev 8:8–9. If the seven seals (Rev 6:1—8:5) have been interpreted to show the faring of the church down through the ages, then the seven trumpets have been interpreted to show the steps in the demise of the Roman empire. Rome was vulnerable toward both land and sea, from which newly developing peoples arrived. Discuss.

3. Read or listen to Rev 8:8–9. Research and tell your findings about the pollution of our oceans and the death of sea creatures and birds. What would result if a third of the world's ships stopped running?

4. Read or listen to Rev 8:8–9. Remember the three protectors during the trumpets: a) prayers (Rev 8:2–5), b) seal of God (Rev 9:4), and c) repentance (Rev 9:20–21). Consider how and why these can protect.

5. Read or listen again to Rev 8:8–9. Do you sense in the trumpets (a) God's revenge (Rev 6:10), (b) God's punishment (Rev 9:20–21), (c) natural consequences (Rev 11:18), or (d) evil from another source? What difference would it make in your life which of these (a, b, c, or d) describes God's character as you understand it?

Prayer Prompt: What means the most to you out of today's reading of Rev 8:8–9? What will you do about it now?

REV 8:10–11

1. When, during your day, are you most thirsty? How would you feel if there was nothing to drink? Share your stories.
2. Read or listen to Rev 8:10–11. Compare Isa 14:12; Luke 10:18; Rev 9:1; 12:3–4; and then Rev 8:12. Sometimes Jesus is called a star, Daystar, Morning Star, but does the star in these readings sound like Jesus or like an enemy of Jesus? Describe the differences.
3. Read or listen to Rev 8:10–11. Research and tell your findings about the pollution of earth's drinking water. Discover some of the chemicals added to our drinking water. Tell what percentage of the world's inhabitants do not have clean drinking water.
4. Read or listen to Rev 8:10–11. Wormwood is the herb that causes abortion. It tastes very bitter. Ponder and discuss: What kind of political or economic pressures would make life very bitter? What kind of system would make abortions popular?
5. Read or listen again to Rev 8:10–11. Compare Rev 22:7; also John 4:14; 7:37–38. Tell how it works for you. How do you turn on the faucet, or dip into the well, or open the flow, for this living water? Tell about a time when you knew you had turned on the flow, or wished you had turned on the flow, of this living water.

Prayer Prompt: What means the most to you out of today's reading of Rev 8:10–11? What will you do about it now?

REV 8:12

1. Do you have a friend or relative with asthma? Please tell others you trust what it is like to feel like you or your friend will never get another full breath of clean air.
2. Read or listen to Rev 8:10–12. Compare this and Rev 9:1, 11 to the dragon of Rev 12:3–4, 9, who drew down a third of the stars of heaven. From these verses collect the names of this star/dragon. Can you also discover what the names mean?
3. Read or listen to Rev 8:12. Research and tell your findings about air and atmospheric pollution on earth. Look for chemicals, waste, smoke, dust, and maybe electronic impulses. What other causes can you think of for the darkening of the lights in the sky?

INVITATIONS TO DISCUSSION 109

4. Read or listen to Rev 8:1–12 in review. Please notice that mention of the targets of the action here are the same as in the creation story of Gen 1: land, oceans, water, air/sky, sun, moon, and stars. Discuss how the actions upon these targets are different from those in Gen 1, and why this might be.

5. Read or listen again to Rev 8:12. Search for sun, moon, and stars in your favorite Bible app, read the texts in context and discuss their meanings. Notice their purpose to rule the days and seasons, and the human tendency to worship them. Notice their use as signs or in meaningful dreams, and their connection to a sign in Rev 12. Discuss.

Prayer Prompt: What means the most to you out of today's reading of Rev 8:12? What will you do about it now?

REV 8:13—9:11

1. What is your experience with suicide ideas, in yourself or in someone you know? Tell someone you trust if you want to.

2. Read or listen to Rev 8:13; 9:1–11; 12:3–4, 9, 12. "Woe" is about horror or terror. Who is this fallen star? Who brings this woe and terror?

3. Read or listen to Rev 9:1–2, 11. The Greek word translated "bottomless pit" is abyss, the same word as used in Luke 8:31 for the place where the demons did not want to go. Read the story of Jesus's mastery over them in Luke 8:26–39. Who do you think would have to give permission if the devil let out all his demons as pictured in Rev 9?

4. Read or listen to Rev 9:4, 11. The name in Greek, Apollyon, means "destroyer." Read Exod 12:21–23 for another story of being protected from the destroyer by the affixing of a special sign. What was the sign made of and where was it placed? Where is the seal of God placed? (Compare Exod 31:13 and Deut 5:15.)

5. Read or listen again to Rev 9:6. Describe the kind of society that might make depression and suicide into an epidemic. List again the three protectors for God's people: Rev 8:4; 9:4, 20. Consider and discuss what might it be about each of these that can protect against suicide.

Prayer Prompt: What means the most to you out of today's reading of Rev 8:13—9:11? What will you do about it now?

REV 9:12-19

1. What have you heard about the seal of God? Discuss and compare your comments with those of your group.
2. Read or listen to Rev 9:12–19. With your Bible app or concordance find in Rev 7–9 all the mentions of "four," "golden," "altar," "heard the number," "horses," "heads," "lions," "breastplates," "mouths," "tails," "power," "hurt." Compare and contrast their settings, ponder their meanings, and mostly let the images wash over you. Share your insights.
3. Read or listen to Rev 9:12–19. List the ways the effect of this sixth trumpet seems worse or more intense that of the fifth. Can you think of any reasons found in the text and context that would make the point of time (or period of time?), mentioned in Rev 9:15 the appropriate time to let loose these angels?
4. Scan Rev 7, 8, and 9. Find mentions of the "seal of God," or "sealed" in their "foreheads." List them in your group, along with what you know so far about the seal of God.
5. Read Exod 20:8–11. An official seal usually includes at least these items: name, realm, and basis of authority. Discover in this commandment these items regarding God. Scan the chapter of Exod 20 to see if these items are included anywhere else in the Ten Commandments. Compare Ezek 20:18–20 to discover how keeping the Sabbath might function as a sign or seal. Discuss.

Prayer Prompt: What means the most to you out of today's reading of Rev 9:12–19? What will you do about it now?

REV 9:20-21

1. Name and write in a list all the things you can think of that sometimes distract your attention or affection away from God.
2. Read or listen to Rev 9:20–21. Three protections during the demise of civilization pictured by the trumpets are prayer (Rev 8:4), the seal of God (Rev 9:4), and repentance (Rev 9:20–21). List the things of which to repent.
3. Read or listen to Rev 9:20. Compare Dan 5:4, 23. Read the context and tell the story in your own words of the demise of this kingdom. Compare also Rev 18:12 and tell what is happening here.

4. Read or listen to Rev 9:21. Compare Exod 20:1–17. What connection might there be between wrong worship and breaking the commandments? Compare also Rev 12:17; 14:12; and 22:14 and tell how important to you are the Ten Commandments.

5. Read or listen to Exod 20:8–11 to discover the Sabbath, as the seal of God, in the midst of the Ten Commandments. Trace and discuss the Bible history of the Sabbath (Gen 2:1–3; 2 Kgs 23:5; Ezek 20:16, 21, 24; Neh 13:17–18; Luke 4:16; 10:25-28; 23:56; 24:1; Acts 13:42; 18:4; Matt 24:20; Isa 66:22–23). Tell how important to you is the Sabbath.

Prayer Prompt: What means the most to you out of today's reading of Rev 9:20–21? What will you do about it now?

REV 10:1–4

1. What is your first reaction when asked to compare and contrast? Discuss the pitfalls and benefits of such activity.

2. Read or listen to Rev 10:1 and compare and contrast this angel with the star seen in Rev 9:1.

3. Read or listen to Rev 10:1–3. Compare and contrast this description with those in Rev 1:15–16; 4:3–5; 5:5–7. The logical question about this angel in Rev 10 lies in our efforts to clearly distinguish between God, Jesus, and the angels. Such clarity and separation is often blurred in the Bible. See Exod 3:1–14.

4. Read or listen to Rev 10:4 and compare and contrast the command to write in Rev 1:19. Discover in Matt 24:35–36, and discuss, the primary thing that we do not know about the future.

5. Read or listen to Rev 10:1–4. Compare and contrast the book opening of Rev 5:1—6:1. Note that, for "book" and "little book," the Greek words are not the same. Also compare and contrast the sealing of the book of Daniel in Dan 12:4. Let us get prepared to have the book of Daniel opened to us now in the time of increased knowledge.

Prayer Prompt: What means the most to you out of today's reading of Rev 10:1–4? What will you do about it now?

REV 10:5-7

1. Tell and discuss instances of seven: days in week, age seven, sevens in Revelation. Compare and discuss instances of six.

2. Read or listen to Rev 10:5-7. Scan Rev 8-11 to notice that Rev 10 is in an interlude between the soundings of the sixth and seventh trumpets. Compare and contrast with this the interlude between the openings of the sixth and seventh seals (Rev 6:1—8:1).

3. Read or listen to Rev 10:5-7. Discover and discuss the first seven in the Bible (Gen 2:1-3), and also 777 (Gen 5:31). Discover and compare the first six in the Bible (Gen 1:24-31), and also 666 (1 Kgs 10:14; 2 Chr 9:14).

4. Read or listen to Rev 10:5-7. Retell and discuss other instances of this language to describe God (Exod 20:11; Neh 9:6; Rev 14:7). What or who is being sworn or sealed or grouped for worship in each case?

5. Read or listen to Rev 10:5-7. What are the two things that will be no longer or be finished? Compare Rev 11:17 to understand the "mystery." Compare Rev 1:3; 12:12; 14:15; 22:10 to understand the "time." We are standing at six, at the edge of seven. Will you get serious with God today?

Prayer Prompt: What means the most to you out of today's reading of Rev 10:5-7? What will you do about it now?

REV 10:8-11

1. When have words flowed easily off your tongue and then you felt sick to your stomach later over their results?

2. Read or listen to Rev 10:8-11. Look up online "Second Great Awakening," and read what you can find about this named period of Christian revival and then disappointment. Some believe Rev 10 refers to the events of this Second Great Awakening. Discuss your findings with your group.

3. Read or listen to Rev 10:8-11. Some believe the "little book" refers to the book of Daniel in the Old Testament. Discover in Dan 8:14 a time period. Use day-for-year reckoning and calculate forward from Daniel's time (ca. 500 BCE) to find an approximate date. Compare this date with your findings in the previous question. Discuss.

4. Read or listen to Rev 10:8–11. Review together the things we have discovered so far in Revelation about church or other enterprises which were promising at first and turned troubling later. Where is the hope in Rev 10:11?

5. Read or listen to Rev 10:8–11. When has reading the Bible been a sweet experience for you? When has it been a bitter experience? Can reading the Bible or feeling God's presence or call be both bitter and sweet at the same time?

Prayer Prompt: What means the most to you out of today's reading of Rev 10:8–11? What will you do about it now?

REV 11:1–2

1. Describe to someone who will listen well some memories you have of being measured.

2. Read or listen to Rev 11:1–2. Compare Ezek 40:3 and Ezek 9:3. Since Rev 11 will have many echoes from Ezekiel, please read Ezek 10:4, 18 and Ezek 43:1–5, and scan anything else in the book that attracts your attention. Then discuss the book's theme and the impact of its being quoted here.

3. Read or listen to Rev 11:1–2. Compare Rev 7:2–3, which introduces the interlude between the sixth and seventh of the seals. Since both Rev 10–11 and Rev 7 are interludes between the sixth and seventh of their groupings, discuss what you might conclude about what happens during the six-to-seven interludes.

4. Read or listen to Rev 11:1–2. Notice the words "temple" and "court" and compare Rev 1:12–13; 6:9; 8:3; 11:19. Research online the furniture and rooms of the Old Testament sanctuary and discuss the meanings of these temple references. What do you think is the difference between temple and court?

5. Read or listen to Rev 11:1–2. Calculate the days and therefore the years in this time period and those found in Rev 11:3; 12:6; 13:5 (compare "times" as years in Dan 7:25 and 4:23, 25, 32). Discuss the general feel of these time periods, whether happy or sad for God's people. Look for the hope in Rev 11.

Prayer Prompt: What means the most to you out of today's reading of Rev 11:1–2? What will you do about it now?

REV 11:3-6

1. Describe to someone who will listen which part of the Bible you like best and why.

2. Read or listen to Rev 11:3-6. Compare the time periods mentioned in Rev 11:2-3. Forty-two months at thirty days per month yields 1260 days. From the context decide and discuss whether these are happy or sad days for God's people.

3. Read or listen to Rev 11:3-4. For "witnesses," compare Rev 12:11 ("testimony" translates the same Greek word as does "witness"). For "olive trees," compare Zech 4:1-14. For "candlesticks," compare Zech 4 and Rev 1:12-13, 20. How are you being a channel through which the light of God comes to the world.

4. Read or listen to Rev 11:5-6. Notice these two are not named though people do connect with them the names of Moses (Exod 7-10, water to blood and plagues) and Elijah (1 Kgs 17-18, drought and fire). Moses and Elijah look to the past and to the future (Mal 4:4-6). Moses initiated the Old Testament; Elijah is the mascot of the New Testament. Discuss.

5. Read or listen to Rev 11:3-6. Research online and make a timeline from the first printing of the Bible, through its translations into the common languages, through the establishment of Bible Societies. What was happening to the Bible in the early 1800s? Tell how many Bibles you have.

Prayer Prompt: What means the most to you out of today's reading of Rev 11:3-6? What will you do about it now?

REV 11:7-13

1. Explain to someone who will listen well how the Bible directs you to Jesus.

2. Read or listen to Rev 11:7-13. Discover and discuss all the echoes, in these verses, of Jesus's life, death, and resurrection on earth. Who is the mastermind behind the aggression in this war?

3. Read or listen to Rev 11:7-13. Research online and other ways the French Revolution, 1789-99. Find the references in history to the church or the Scriptures. Describe how the ways in which the Bible

was treated in Paris are similar to the ways Jesus was treated. Focus especially on the echoes of Jesus's life and death in these verses.

4. Read or listen to Rev 11:13. Research online and other ways the Lisbon Earthquake, November 1, 1755. Compare Rev 9:20–21 and ponder why the reaction of the remnant left alive was different in these two instances.

5. Read or listen to Rev 11:11–12. Read also and compare Ezek 37:1–14. Describe and discuss in your group the Bible's waxing or waning vitality in your own life's timeline. Would you be willing today to pray together for increased power of the Holy Spirit in your life and group, your street and church? The Holy Spirit will make the Bible come alive for you and show you Jesus.

Prayer Prompt: What means the most to you out of today's reading of Rev 11:7–13? What will you do about it now?

REV 11:14–15

1. Tell someone who will listen well about something bad in your life that turned out to be good.

2. Read or listen to Rev 11:14–15. Review together the first two woes (Rev 8:13; 9:12): demons like scorpions with tails with which to hurt, and horses with serpent tails and mouths with which to kill. Review together the three protections (Rev 8:4; 9:4, 20–21): prayer, Sabbath, and repentance.

3. Read or listen to Rev 11:14–15. Review together the seven angels with trumpets sounding (Rev 8–9). Notice the progressive demise of environment and civilization. Then review the opening of the seven seals (Rev 6:1—8:1). Notice the life cycle of projects, churches, civilizations. Discuss.

4. Read or listen to Rev 11:14–15. Review and compare the interludes between the sixth and seventh of these sets of seven (that is, compare Rev 7 with 10–11). Discuss whether you think the interludes are hopeful or full of more bad news.

5. Read or listen to Rev 11:14–15. Now focus on Rev 10–11. What can you find to learn from this interlude about living through a time when food, water, and air sources are poisoned and the humane impulses of people toward one another break down into chaos? Hint: Read Rev

10:11; 11:11, plus Rev 7:16–17. List some practical actions you can take in the midst of trouble.

Prayer Prompt: What means the most to you out of today's reading of Rev 11:14–15? What will you do about it now?

REV 11:15-19

1. Review steps you have taken, decisions you have made, or stages you have passed through on your life journey so far.
2. Read or listen to Rev 11:15–19. Compare and contrast the praise segments in Rev 11:15 and in Rev 11:17. Discuss what you might find as their common theme. To whom is each directed?
3. Read or listen to Rev 11:15. Compare and contrast the seventh stage in the groups of seven seen so far (Rev 3:14–22; 8:1–5; 11:15–19). Tell where you see yourself in each instance.
4. Read or listen to Rev 11:18. List the segments of this reading, then scan ahead in Revelation. Some see in Rev 11:18 an outline of the rest of the book of Revelation. Some also see in Rev 11:18 a recap of important ideas already mentioned. Discuss what you find in scanning.
5. Read or listen to Rev 11:19. Review temple imagery in Revelation and discuss any order or progression that you find (Rev 1:12; 6:9; 8:3; 11:19; 21:3–22). Read Deut 10:1–5 to learn what is in this ark of the testimony. Discuss why you think this would show up here, at this position, in the book of Revelation.

Prayer Prompt: What means the most to you out of today's reading of Rev 11:15–19? What will you do about it now?

REV 12:1-2

1. Tell about a moment of wonder you experienced as a child of age nine or ten.
2. Read or listen to Rev 11:19—12:2. Remember the ark of the testament on earth, and how there was only one day in the year when the ark was available to be seen by the priest. This was the day of atonement, Yom Kippur, the day of justice and of new life. How is this Old Testament event a good setting here for the wonders in the heavens?

3. Read or listen to Rev 12:1–2. Compare Isa 54:5–6 and Song 6:9–10. The woman might represent Eve, Mary, and, by extension, all Israel, or all the church. Prophets wrote of Israel as the beloved, betrothed, and bride of God. Share what you observe.

4. Read or listen to Rev 12:1–2. Compare Gen 37:9–11, where Jacob immediately interpreted sun, moon, and twelve stars as his mother, father, and brothers, the people of Israel. Would that interpretation fit, or bring additional breadth, here?

5. Read or listen to Rev 12:1–2. Compare Isa 66:6–9, John 16:21–22. The fear and pain and hope of childbirth are used in the Old Testament to picture the time of the Messiah and in the New Testament to picture the time of his return. Tell your group your current feelings about Jesus's return.

Prayer Prompt: What means the most to you out of today's reading of Rev 12:1–2? What will you do about it now?

REV 12:3–4

1. Tell about your first, or most memorable, experience with a snake.

2. Read or listen to Rev 12:3–4. Compare Rev 12:9 to discover some other names by which this dragon is called. Read Gen 3:1–15 to find the serpent's characteristics and actions in the beginning. Compare Rev 6:4 to think about what the word "red" might indicate as a descriptor of this dragon. Describe and discuss the character of this dragon.

3. Read or listen to Rev 12:3–4. How many heads, and how many horns are there? Read Gen 2:1–2 and Exod 20:8–11 to try to understand what the number seven would indicate. Consider the differences in use between a head and a horn.

4. Read or listen to Rev 12:3–4. Compare Exod 34:28 and Rev 17:3, 12 to try to understand what the number ten would indicate. Notice, are the crowns (these are kingly crowns) on the heads or on the horns?

5. Read or listen to Rev 12:3–4. Compare Matt 2:13–18 to discover who was waiting to destroy Jesus when he was born. Review Gen 3:15 and discuss why the serpent would want to destroy Jesus.

Prayer Prompt: What means the most to you out of today's reading of Rev 12:3–4? What will you do about it now?

REV 12:5-6

1. Tell your group of a memory you hold surrounding a birth.
2. Read or listen to Rev 12:1–5. Let the pictures in this reading wash over your mind. Read it again, then read it yet again. Where is Jesus in this reading? The word "rule" in Rev 12:5 is the word for "shepherd" or "pastor." Compare with Rev 2:27 and 19:15, and discuss.
3. Read or listen to Rev 12:1–5. The woman, Mary (Matt 2:16) and Israel (Isa 54), gave birth to the Messiah in face of hostility from the dragon (Satan and Rome). The entire life of Jesus is contained in Rev 12:5 (Matt 1:1 to Acts 1:11). Retell or reenact, with your group, some part of the life of Jesus.
4. Read or listen to Rev 12:5. Compare Gen 3:15 and discuss how Jesus's heel was bruised and Satan's head was bruised in the event of Jesus presence and acts on earth. Check ahead in Rev 12:10–11 (KJV) for mention of the "blood of the Lamb" and the "accuser cast down."
5. Read or listen to Rev 12:6. The woman, God's people, now including gentiles (Rom 11), goes where? What happens to her? For how long (compare Rev 11:3 and 13:5)? Please note divine provision and nurture in the midst of the devil's hostility (compare and reenact 1 Kgs 17:1—18:1).

Prayer Prompt: What means the most to you out of today's reading of Rev 12:5-6? What will you do about it now?

REV 12:7-9

1. Discuss the differences between a civil war and a war of aggression or defense between or among nations.
2. Read or listen to Rev 12:7–9. Notice the similarity of this reading with Rev 12:3–4. Discuss whether you think this is an instance of recapitulation or of new developments, the same time, or years apart. Be sure to check the context and give biblical or historical evidence for your thinking.
3. Read or listen to Rev 12:7–9. Compare the other scriptural instances of Michael (Dan 10:13, 21; 12:1; Jude 1:9). Describe the powers of this being and compare them to those of Jesus.

4. Read or listen to Rev 12:7–9. List the names of the devil. Discuss the meanings or connotations of each name (including meanings like accuser and deceiver). What is the difference to life here between, on the one hand, believing there is a real person with these characteristics and, on the other hand, believing there is no person and only these evil characteristics at work?

5. Read or listen to Rev 12:7–9. Who is the stronger in the great war? How can you link up with the winning side?

Prayer Prompt: What means the most to you out of today's reading of Rev 12:7–9? What will you do about it now?

REV 12:10-12

1. Tell of a time you experienced slander or accusation. How do you feel about it now? Listen to other such stories in your group.

2. Read or listen to Rev 12:10–12. Compare the devil's power of accusation with Christ's power to champion your cause. Is the devil's anger and cunning increasing or decreasing? Read Job 1:6–12 and discuss the devil's motives for accusation.

3. Read or listen to Rev 12:11. Though the devil is a well-conquered foe, humans and human institutions still need to overcome his remaining presence on earth. What does it mean to you in real life to overcome him "by the blood of the Lamb"? Compare Rev 7:14, and discuss.

4. Read or listen to Rev 12:11. What does it mean to you in real life to overcome the devil by the word of your testimony or witness? Picture a courtroom with God the judge, Jesus your lawyer, and Satan the prosecutor. What does it mean to witness, or give testimony? Compare Rev 1:9; 6:9; 12:17; 19:10; Acts 1:8; Isa 43:10–12; 44:8–9, and discuss.

5. Read or listen to Rev 12:11. How does "loved not their lives unto the death" (Rev 12:11 KJV) relate to the other two clauses in Rev 12:11? To human overcoming? To your life now, here?

Prayer Prompt: What means the most to you out of today's reading of Rev 12:10–12? What will you do about it now?

REV 12:13-16

1. Which would you call yourself, introvert or extrovert? Talk and listen in your group to different ways these are experienced.
2. Read or listen to Rev 12:13-16. Without working hard to interpret, describe two things the dragon did against the woman. Now let Revelation explain itself, and in Rev 17:15 discover what water represents, then describe again what the dragon did against the woman, the people of Jesus.
3. Read or listen to Rev 12:14. In Exod 19:4, find a picture of Israel going to the desert out of Egypt. In Isa 40:31, find a similar picture of God's people. In 1 Kgs 17:1, 5-6 and Jas 5:17, find a picture of Elijah in drought and discover how long the drought lasted. Compare and discuss these Old Testament stories.
4. Read or listen to Rev 12:14. Compare the time periods mentioned in Rev 11:2-3 and in Dan 7:25. The specific concurring times would suggest looking for a historical period of church development lasting more than one thousand years during the Middle Ages.
5. Read or listen to Rev 12:16. Compare Exod 15:12 and Num 16:1-3, 32-33. If water is crowds of people, then what things during the Middle Ages and later created population control on earth? Read Isa 43:1-2, and tell how God has helped you in a time of fear among many people.

Prayer Prompt: What means the most to you out of today's reading of Rev 12:13-16? What will you do about it now?

REV 12:17

1. How many of your cousins and other relatives do you know? What is left of the earliest generation alive in your family? That is the "remnant" of that generation.
2. Read or listen to Rev 12:17. Who is the dragon (Rev 12:9)? Why is he angry (Rev 12:12)? Who is the woman (Rev 12:1-2, 5-6)?
3. Read or listen to Rev 12:17. What two things do the people of God do and have that especially draw the dragon's anger toward those who are left? Compare and contrast, by reading contexts, other places where these two things are mentioned (Ps 19:7; Isa 8:16-20).

4. Read or listen to Rev 12:17. Compare Rev 14:12 and 22:14. List, compare, and discuss the consequences and benefits of keeping the commandments of God. Bonus: Compare Dan 7:25 and consider and discuss the consequences of trying to change God's laws.

5. Read or listen to Rev 12:17. Compare Rev 1:2, 9; 6:9; 11:3; 12:11; 15:5; 19:10. List, compare, and discuss the consequences and benefits of having the testimony, or witness, of Jesus. Bonus: Compare John 5:39; Luke 24:48; and Acts 1:8 to consider and discuss the source and power of this testimony.

Prayer Prompt: What means the most to you out of today's reading of Rev 12:17? What will you do about it now?

REV 12:17, AGAIN

1. Tell and discuss in group some of the family commandments with which you were raised.

2. Read or listen to Rev 12:17. Who is the dragon? Why is he angry? Who is the woman? What two things do the people of God do and have?

3. Read or listen to Rev 12:17. Who wrote the Ten Commandments (Exod 34:28; Deut 4:13; 5:22; 10:4)? Where were they kept (Deut 10:1–5, 10)? What was kept and later found in the side of that place (Deut 31:26; Josh 24:26; 2 Kgs 22:8; 2 Chr 34:14–15)?

4. Read or listen to Rev 12:17. How did Israel react to the Ten Commandments at Horeb (Exod 19:8; 24:3–7; 32:1–35)? In Canaan (Josh 24:1–31; 2 Kgs 23:1–5)? Around the tomb of Jesus (Luke 23:54—24:1)?

5. Read or listen to Rev 12:17. According to Jesus, what was the law (Matt 19:16–19; 22:35–40; Luke 10:25–28; compare Matt 5:17–48)? According to Paul, what was the law (Rom 7:7–8; 13:8–10)? After human broken promises, what was the promise of God regarding the law (Jer 31:31–35; Ezek 36:22–27; Heb 8:6–13; 10:15–18)? Discuss what relation love has to the law. Are you accepting Jesus's love for you today?

Prayer Prompt: What means the most to you out of today's reading of Rev 12:17? What will you do about it now?

REV 12:17, THIRD TIME

1. Have you ever been sworn in as a witness in court? Or have you given recommendation for someone? Tell about it.
2. Read or listen to Rev 12:17. Who is the dragon? Why is he angry? Who is the woman? What two things do the people of God do and have?
3. Read or listen to Rev 12:17. Read Rev 19:10 and tell, What is the testimony of Jesus? Read Rev 11:19 and tell, to which article of furniture is it connected? What was kept in that piece of furniture (Deut 10:1–5, 10)?
4. Read or listen to Rev 12:17. Read Joel 2:28–29 and 1 Cor 12:1–11 to discover and discuss how the Spirit is connected to prophecy. Read Ezek 36:26–27 and Heb 10:15–18 to discuss how the Spirit is connected to the commandments. Bonus: Read 1 Sam 10:10–12; 19:20–24 and discuss what you think was happening here between the spirit and prophecy.
5. Read or listen to Rev 12:17. Read 2 Chr 20. In your group, retell or draw or dramatize the story of 2 Chr 20. Tell, and listen to others tell, Where are you in the story? Read together, aloud, the message sent through the prophet to the people in 2 Chr 20:15–17, 20.

Prayer Prompt: What means the most to you out of today's reading of Rev 12:17? What will you do about it now?

REV 13:1

1. Tell about your last frightening or disturbing dream. Did you attach meaning to it? Listen to others tell of theirs.
2. Read or listen to Rev 13:1. Compare and contrast the creature described here with the dragon described in Rev 12:3, 9, 17. Note the numbers of the heads, horns, and crowns as well as the placement of the crowns. Picture and ponder.
3. Read or listen to Rev 13:1. Compare and contrast this creature with the one described in Dan 7:7, 19. Bring the dragon of Rev 12:3, 8, 17 into your comparison. Notice heads, horns, and crowns and what it does with the remnant or residue.

4. Read or listen to Rev 13:1. Compare Dan 7:3, to consider this creature's origin from the sea. Read and make notes about Gen 1:10; Job 9:8; 26:7–12; 38:8; Ps 77:19; 89:9; 95:3–5; and Rev 17:15 to discover and discuss what the sea may have meant to John's first readers.

5. Read or listen to Rev 13:1. Review the work we did some time ago in discussing the relationship Daniel may have to Revelation. Consider Dan 12:4, 9–10; Matt 24:15; Rev 10:2, 8–10. Will you commit to reading both Daniel and Revelation now, reading them in light of each other?

Prayer Prompt: What means the most to you out of today's reading of Rev 13:1? What will you do about it now?

REV 13:1–8

1. Tell about a project you did or helped, that turned out unprofitable or hurtful. Were you able to turn it around?

2. Read or listen to Rev 13:1–8. Make a list of recurring words. These are the key words, and they give clues to the organization of the section. This is the reason to notice their placement. The placement of the word, "worship," identifies two recapitulating segments to this section. What limitations happen to the creature preceding the worship?

3. Read or listen to Rev 13:1–8. Notice also "blasphemy" and "mouth." Always notice the root word and all its other forms (noun, verb, adjective, plural, etc.). Notice also "war" and "saints" and compare this with Rev 12:17. Share what you learned.

4. Read or listen to Rev 13:1–8. Notice the word "give." List the things given to this creature. Who gave them?

5. Read or listen to Rev 13:1–8. Compare Dan 7:1–28. How many instances of three or more consecutive words can you find similar between these two readings? List them and discuss what might be the meaning of the similarities. Bonus: Read also Dan 2:28–45, which is considered by most scholars to be the precursor to recapitulation in Dan 7:1–28. Discover and discuss the similarities here. Ask Jesus to help you understand, as Jesus suggested in Matt 24:15.

Prayer Prompt: What means the most to you out of today's reading of Rev 13:1–8? What will you do about it now?

REV 13:9-10

1. On a scale of 1–10, how well did you do this week at listening respectfully to someone who disagreed with you? Tell about the experience if you wish to.
2. Read or listen to Rev 13:9–10. "Let the one who has an ear, hear" (Rev 13:9 KJV, WZ paraphrase). Locate seven other instances of this sentence in Rev 2 and 3. What function did this sentence serve there? Read and discuss the contexts and placements of Jesus's similar sentence in Matt 13:9, 43. Consider and discuss what function this sentence serves here in Rev 13.
3. Read or listen to Rev 13:9–10. Compare with Exod 22:21–24. How fair do you consider reversal as a reward or punishment?
4. Read or listen to Rev 13:9–10. Compare the four mentions of patience in Rev 2:2–3, 19, and Rev 3:10, with this mention of patience. Then compare this with the mention in Rev 14:12. Discuss what you learned. Bonus: Include Jesus's words in Luke 21:19, 34, with their contexts, in your comparisons on patience.
5. Read or listen to Rev 13:1–10. Summarize and describe as well as you can what is happening in these verses. List and tell identifying factors that could help a person know the character of this animal.

Prayer Prompt: What means the most to you out of today's reading of Rev 13:9–10? What will you do about it now?

REV 13:11-14

1. List and describe the changes in information technology that have happend during your lifetime. Bigger? Smaller? Power differential?
2. Read or listen to Rev 13:11–14. Compare the origins of the two animals (Rev 13:1, 11). Compare Rev 21:1 and Rev 12:16 and discuss what must have been the general feelings brought up by each designation of origin.
3. Read or listen to Rev 13:11–12. Describe the two animals, the one the second one looked like, and the one he spoke like. Compare Rev 5:5–6, 12; 12:3–4, 17 with this second animal in Rev 13. Discuss the difference between a Lion-Lamb and a Lamb-Dragon.

INVITATIONS TO DISCUSSION 125

4. Read or listen to Rev 13:11–14. Get the whole story from the Old Testament, of fire from heaven, in 1 Kgs 18. Expand your reading to 1 Kgs 17–19. Read several times and discuss the possible effects of this memory both on people reading Revelation and on the dragon, Satan.

5. Read or listen to Rev 13:11–14. Compare and contrast the characteristics and worship patterns of this animal with those of the animal described in Rev 13:1–8. Consider and discuss various uses and connotations of the word "image" ("icon" in Greek). Read Exod 20:4–6 and decide again whom you will worship.

Prayer Prompt: What means the most to you out of today's reading of Rev 13:11–14? What will you do about it now?

REV 13:11–18

1. On a full sheet of paper make a table with columns and rows. Across the top, label the columns for the animals: Dragon from the sky, Animal from the sea, Animal from the earth, Image. When was the last time you made a table? Or an image?

2. Read or listen to Rev 13:11–18. Compare Rev 12–13 and Dan 2 and 7. Start populating your table by listing characteristics on the left side and marking the column for which animal has that characteristic. Look for these at least: 1) Dragon-like, 2) Blasphemy, 3) Makes war, 4) Attacks the remnant or residue, 5) Wounded and healed, 6) People wondered and worshiped, 7) Assumes to change God's times and laws, 8) 1260 days, 42 months, 3½ years, 9) Miracles of sight, 10) Plans executions, 11) Economic sanctions, 12) Named or measured by sixes (Dan 3:1; Rev 13:18).

3. Read or listen to Rev 13:16–18. Trace and describe the grammatical relationships here between mark, name, and number.

4. Read or listen to Rev 13:18. Compare 2 Chr 9:13 and Gen 1:1—2:4. Discuss everything you can imagine about Old Testament echoes around the number 6.

5. Read or listen to Rev 13:18. Where is Jesus? Look for him in wisdom (see 1 Cor 1:30), and in understanding (see Matt 24:15).

Prayer Prompt: What means the most to you out of today's reading of Rev 13:11–18? What will you do about it now?

REV 14:1-5

1. Think about and discuss what it would mean to have only pure truth in what you say or hear, no trolling or entrapment, no "little white lies," no political lies, no lies to oneself. If you say it cannot be done, try imagining it anyway and discuss the feelings aroused by the experience.
2. Read or listen to Rev 14:1–5. List and discuss the characteristics of the Lamb. Compare Rev 5.
3. Read or listen to Rev 14:1–5. List and discuss the characteristics (not the identity) of the 144,000. Compare Rev 7.
4. Read or listen to Rev 14:1–5. Compare Rom 11. Review and describe what has happened in Revelation between Rev 7 and Rev 14. List the allusions to Israel in these chapters.
5. Read or listen to Rev 14:1–5. Compare Rev 13. Notice (1) the deceit and lack of it, (2) the people's voice and lack of it, (3) the mark and the name in the forehead, and (4) the numbers 144,000 and 666. Bonus: Compare Rev 2:20–22 and 12:1–2 to discover the difference between a woman who can "defile" a person and a woman who carries purity.

Prayer Prompt: What means the most to you out of today's reading of Rev 14:1–5? What will you do about it now?

REV 14:6-7

1. What do you know about angels? How do you know it? How many different angels do you find in reading Revelation so far? Tell your group.
2. Read or listen to Rev 14:6–7. Here is another angel (compare Heb 1:13–14). Where is he flying? For whom is his message? In your own words, what is the gospel? What is everlasting about it (compare Dan 7:14, 27)?
3. Read or listen to Rev 14:6–7. List the three calls to action that make up this urgent message. Describe them in your own words and discuss what they might mean in today's world. (For the word "fear" compare Deut 6:2; Eccl 12:13–14; Prov 9:10.)
4. Read or listen to Rev 14:6–7. Discover at the end of this reading the identifying reason humans are called to worship this God. Compare

Exod 20:8–11 (also Neh 9:6; Ps 69:34; 96:11; 135:6; 146:6; Acts 4:24; 14:15; Rev 5:13; 10:6).

5. Read or listen to Rev 14:6–7. Find in the middle of Rev 14:7 the time-sensitive reason humans are called to fear God and give God glory (compare Dan 7:9–10; Acts 24:25). Bonus: Compare Dan 7 with Rev 13–14, looking for four animals, ten horns, another thing, and then the judgment, followed by the coming of the (a) Son of man.

Prayer Prompt: What means the most to you out of today's reading of Rev 14:6–7? What will you do about it now?

REV 14:8

1. Tell when you first discovered the fun of cross-referencing in your Bible. Share various ways of keeping the notes. Discuss how the first hearers would have had those Bible memories deep in their personalities and what that might mean for interpretation.
2. Read or listen to Rev 14:8. If this is the second angel, which would have been the first? Review his message. Can you find the third? Is there a fourth or more in this series?
3. Read or listen to Rev 14:8. Read also the story in Gen 11:1–9. Draw or dramatize this story of the origins of the name Babylon. What are the principles about God and humans that are available to us in this reading?
4. Read or listen to Rev 14:8. Read also and compare Isa 14:3–15. Who is speaking this proverb against Babylon and why? Discuss the characteristics of Babylon noted here. Compare Isa 21:6–9. Compare and share.
5. Read or listen to Rev 14:8. Compare Dan 4. Discuss what the king of Babylon did and said that got him in trouble with God. Bonus: Preview Rev 17–18 looking for hints about the character and other aspects of this Babylon. Compare also Rev 16:13, 19.

Prayer Prompt: What means the most to you out of today's reading of Rev 14:8? What will you do about it now?

REV 14:9-11

1. Have you known of a person, plant, or animal who died of a parasite? Discuss what kinds of things live by infesting and starving, overtaking, or out-bursting their host: Cancer, worms, larvae, lice, technology hackers, social media trolls, etc. Discuss what humans usually do with such parasites and why.
2. Read or listen to Rev 14:9-11. Reread the antecedent to Rev 14:9 in 13:13-16, and its counterpart in 14:1-5. List and match the phrases that describe two opposite verbal pictures. Discuss and improve your lists.
3. Read or listen to Rev 14:9-11. Compare Rev 14:10 with Rev 14:8. What different things might the two cups represent?
4. Read or listen to Rev 14:9-11. List the phrases that are often used to picture righteous enjoyment in the ongoing torture and torment of others. Now read Gen 18:1-2, 20-33; 19:24-28, finding the "fire and brimstone (sulfur)," "the presence of the holy angels, and the presence of the Lamb," and "smoke ascending" in the story of the fall of Sodom and Gomorrah. Then read Jude 1:7 and ponder whether those cities are still burning, as an example to us. Read Isa 63:9 and 2 Pet 3:9 to find out if God enjoys making trouble or death for anyone.
5. Read or listen to Rev 14:9-11. Compare Rev 14:6-7, noticing that the theme that is common to both angels is "worship." What, in your daily life, constitutes worship? Is it clear to you and those who watch you to whom you are giving the worship?

Prayer Prompt: What means the most to you out of today's reading of Rev 14:9-11? What will you do about it now?

REV 14:12

1. Think of a clean joke that has three parts and tell it so you can enjoy it together as a group. Notice together the value and function of each of the three parts.
2. Read or listen to Rev 14:12. Compare Rev 12:17 (also Rev 19:10) and list three gifts that the people of God hold. Discuss how these might compare with the three offers from Jesus in Rev 3:14-22? Maybe start a chart of threes.

INVITATIONS TO DISCUSSION 129

3. Read or listen to Rev 14:12. Notice that this is the concluding sentence of what the three angels announced in the midst of the sky for all people. Summarize each of the three messages: First, worship God; Second, self-worship fails; Third, there will be a test. What other threes do you remember from the Bible?

4. Read or listen to Rev 14:12. Find and read these other threes in prophecy and compare their meanings: (a) Throne scenes, Rev 4; Dan 7; Rev 20; (b) How to overcome, Rev 12:11; (c) Decrees against God, Dan 3, 6; Rev 13; (d) Forces against God, Rev 16:13; 12:1–17; 13:1–10, 11–18.

5. Read or listen to Rev 14:12. Now find some other threes in the Bible and compare their meanings to the messages of the three angels: (a) The Lord's requirements according to Micah (Mic 6:8); (b) Jesus's temptation (Matt 4:1–11); (c) Prayer (Matt 7:7); (d) Who Jesus is (John 14:6); (e) Paul's picture of the church (1 Cor 6:19–20; 2 Cor 6:16–18; 1 Cor 3:16–23). Bonus: Find the three messages in each of these stories: Elijah (1 Kgs 18); Jehoshaphat (2 Chron 20:1–25); Wilderness sanctuary (Exod 25–27).

Prayer Prompt: What means the most to you out of today's reading of Rev 14:12? What will you do about it now?

REV 14:13

1. As a child where did you go when you were tired? Tell someone who will listen and then listen to that person tell.

2. Read or listen to Rev 14:13. Please notice the timing notation, "henceforth," meaning from now on, or after this time. Compare the timing notation in Rev 14:7. Ponder what would make this material timely in John's day. In what other era of history might this be timely?

3. Read or listen to Rev 14:13. Compare Rev 12–14 with Dan 7. Find the lion-bear-leopard-dragon, then the judgment, then the coming of the son of man here at the center of each book. Ponder the ordering and timing of these pieces. Discuss what might the one thousand two hundred and sixty days, three and one-half years, forty-two months, have to do with the timing notations in Rev 14:7, 13.

4. Read or listen to Rev 14:13. Compare 1 Thess 4:16 and its context for more depth on the expression "die in the Lord." Compare Heb 4:9–11

and its context for more depth on the expressions "rest" and "works." Discuss.

5. Read or listen to Rev 14:13. Compare Eph 2:5–9; Titus 3:5; Matt 16:27; Rev 18:6; 20:12–13. Ponder and discuss what is the significance of the works following them rather than going before them into judgment? Glance at Rev 2:2, 9, 13, 19; 3:1, 8, 15 to confirm and discuss what God knows about each of us.

Prayer Prompt: What means the most to you out of today's reading of Rev 14:13? What will you do about it now?

REV 14:14-20

1. Name one thing you hated sorting as a child and tell why. Then name one thing you loved sorting as a child and tell why.

2. Read or listen to Rev 14:14–20. Describe the two groups pictured here and tell their futures in your own words. Discover where the angel announcing the grape harvest comes from and ponder why that might be significant, Rev 6:9–11. Describe the feelings these pictures arouse in you.

3. Read or listen to Rev 14:14–20. Where is Jesus among these pictures? Compare Matt 24:30–31 and John 5:22. Tell whether and why or why not you like the Jesus pictured here.

4. Read or listen to Rev 14:14–20. Recall or review these other two-path-two-destinies stories and discuss how this serves as a theme, paradigm, or rhetorical device in the Bible. Prov 7–8; Matt 7:24–27; 21:28–31; 25:1–13. How was the choice made clear and the destiny delivered in these stories?

5. Read or listen to Rev 14:14–20. Review these additional two-path-two-destinies stories, especially noting who gets to sort the path-takers and deliver the destinies. Matt 7:13–14; 13:24–30; 25:31–46; John 5:28–29. Can you trust Jesus to know you well enough with love to be grateful Jesus sits on the judgment throne and no one else?

Prayer Prompt: What means the most to you out of today's reading of Rev 14:14–20? What will you do about it now?

REV 15:1-4

1. For what "great and marvelous" works toward you would you like to praise God today? Tell someone.
2. Read or listen to Rev 15:1-4. What are the other two "signs in heaven" that came before this one (Rev 12:1-3)? What might be the connections between these signs?
3. Read or listen to Rev 15:1-4. Can you discover two different reasons these might be called the seven "last" plagues? See Exod 8:22; 9:4, 6, 26; 10:23; 11:7; 12:13. See also Rev 9:20; 11:6.
4. Read or listen to Rev 15:1-4. Draw, rap, or poeticize the victorious scene pictured here. Remember to include the sea of glass and the harps of God. Perhaps include also the means to this victory found in Rev 12:11.
5. Read or listen to Rev 15:1-4. Where is Jesus in this reading? Would you say the Lamb is (a) literally Jesus with wool and four legs, (b) representing Jesus like a mascot, (c) a characterization of Jesus, or (d) just a symbol, or another name, to be translated immediately into Jesus? Bonus: Read the song of Moses in Exod 15 and a psalm of Moses in Ps 90. Ponder this song in Rev 15 being called the song of Moses and the Lamb. What does it hold in common with the other songs of Moses? Do you know of a song of the Lamb?

Prayer Prompt: What means the most to you out of today's reading of Rev 15:1-4? What will you do about it now?

REV 15:5-8

1. Did you ever burn something you were cooking so much that the pan or kettle was ruined? Tell your group about that event.
2. Read or listen to Rev 15:5-8. Find the opening of the temple in heaven (Rev 11:19) and then find, list, and describe the angels that came out of the temple in Rev 14 and 15. Check Num 1:50 for the tabernacle on earth and its servers.
3. Read or listen to Rev 15:7. Scan the throne scene in Rev 4 to discover the role of the four living creatures. Then compare Rev 5:8 with 15:7. There were golden cups, bowls, basins, or vials. Compare and discuss how many there were and of what they were full.

4. Read or listen to Rev 15:7. The first readers would have remembered the temple service utensils. Follow their history (Exod 25:29; 27:3; 2 Kgs 25:15; Dan 1:2; 5:3). What reasons can you imagine for the mention and use of these here?

5. Read or listen to Rev 15:5–8. Compare the filling of the temple with the glory of God at these previous times: Exod 40:34–35; 1 Kgs 8:10–11; 2 Chr 5:13–14. With the linen clothing of the angels and the "no man may enter" exclusion, this scene would also remind the first readers of Yom Kippur, the Day of Atonement, of Lev 16 (especially Lev 16:4, 17). Can you tell where is Jesus?

Prayer Prompt: What means the most to you out of today's reading of Rev 15:5–8? What will you do about it now?

REV 16:1–2

1. What feelings come up when you think about the future? Talk and listen to each other about these feelings.

2. Read or listen to Rev 16:1–2. Scan Rev 16:1–9 and then review the trumpets in Rev 8:6–12. Notice the similarities and differences between the trumpets and the plagues. The first four trumpets describe natural phenomena, and we cited pollution in soil, ocean, water, and air. The first four plagues affect totalities in natural phenomena, and they are more clearly connected with choices of worship.

3. Read or listen to Rev 16:1–2. Compare Exod 9:8–11. Scan the context there to understand the role of the magicians in Pharoah's court and how their sores connected to their obstructions to God's plan.

4. Read or listen to Rev 16:1–2. Compare Ps 91:1–4. Scan that context to notice the many promises to those who trust God amid surrounding plagues.

5. Read or listen to Rev 16:1–2. What two facts identify those who receive this plague? You can review this mark and image of the beast in Rev 13:14–18; 14:9–11; 15:1–4. How might a boil, ulcer, or some other sore be a fitting consequence of accepting a mark or worshiping an image? Whom will you worship today?

Prayer Prompt: What means the most to you out of today's reading of Rev 16:1–2? What will you do about it now?

REV 16:3-7

1. List together some ways in which life would be different if there were no water on earth.

2. Read or listen to Rev 16:3-7. Read also Exod 7:17-21 and Rev 8:8-11. Egypt's River Nile was an object of worship. The trumpets come before for the full unmasking of false worship in Rev 12-14. Retell the stories and contexts of these other plagues on water, noting the extent of damage for each.

3. Read or listen to Rev 16:3-7. (Compare the war and killing in Rev 12:17; 13:15.) Would you describe this plague as a case of natural consequences? What might be the significance of the angel of the waters and the voices from the altar (see Rev 6:10) joining to say God's ways are true and just? Is this then understandable consequences?

4. Read or listen to Rev 16:3-7. Read again 7:14-17. Though these people have an intimate relationship with blood, also, they have plenty of water to drink. What makes them different?

5. Read or listen to Rev 16:3-7. In Rev 3:1-4, find another group referred to as "they are worthy." Discuss the similarities and differences. In which group will you be?

Prayer Prompt: What means the most to you out of today's reading of Rev 16:13-7? What will you do about it now?

REV 16:8-11

1. List together some ways in which life would be different if there were no sunlight on earth, let us say, for two weeks.

2. Read or listen to Rev 16:8-11. Notice the mention of their sores. Review all that has happened since the sores first appeared: Sores because they had the mark. Blood in sea and rivers because they shed the blood of God's people. No cleansing or drinking water. Now scorching sun to increase the drought, and then darkness. How do the people respond?

3. Read or listen to Rev 16:8-11. Consider the origins and prevalence of sun worship. Look up Deut 4:19; 17:3; 2 Kgs 23:5; Jer 8:2; Ezek 8:16; and online religious information on Egypt and Babylon. How might the fourth and fifth plagues be understandable consequences?

4. Read or listen to Rev 16:8-11. Compare Rev 8:12—9:2, the fourth and fifth trumpets, affecting the sun only partially. Read Rev 9:20-21 and compare this reaction to that noted in Rev 16:9, 11.

5. Read or listen to Rev 16:8-11. Compare and discuss Exod 10:21-24. Scan the next few chapters in Exodus to learn what event followed this plague of darkness, and what preparations God's people made to be safe.

Prayer Prompt: What means the most to you out of today's reading of Rev 16:8-11? What will you do about it now?

REV 16:12

1. Research the geographical area around the Euphrates River and tell your group what you learned.

2. Read or listen to Rev 16:12. Scan three sets of seven in Revelation (Seals, Rev 6:1—8:1; Trumpets, Rev 8:6—11:19; and Plagues, Rev 16:1-21). How does the amount of word space given to the sixth increment differ from that given to all the other increments? Discuss what significance this finding might have.

3. Read or listen to Rev 16:12. The Euphrates River is associated in the Bible with Babylon and the Nile River with Egypt. Babylon is where the people of Israel were held in exile and Egypt is where the people of Israel were held in slavery. Discuss the similarities and differences between these two.

4. Read or listen to Rev 16:12. Compare 2 Chr 36:22-23; Isa 41:2, 24-28; 43:15-16; 44:27-28; 45:1, 13, 18; Jer 50:38; 51:13, 36-37. List and discuss the similarities in the stories of Cyrus with the pictures in Rev 16:13. Discuss what place the expected fall of Babylon may have had in the emotions of the people of Israel.

5. Read or listen to Rev 16:12. Read also Dan 1:1-6, 21; 5:1-31; 6:28; 10:1. Retell the story of the fall of Babylon. What do you think were the causes of its fall?

Prayer Prompt: What means the most to you out of today's reading of Rev 16:12? What will you do about it now?

REV 16:13-14

1. Tell a story from your childhood about a frog, or research and tell the life cycle of a frog.

2. Read or listen to Rev 16:13-14. There are at least four stories of Jesus and unclean spirits. One was in church (Mark 1:23-27), another among the graves (Mark 5:2-13), another in the midst of bigoted nationalism (Mark 7:24-30), and another had the disciples stumped (Luke 9:38-42; Matt 17:14-21). Discuss what happened to the unclean spirit in all these instances.

3. Read or listen to Rev 16:13-14. Retell the story in the Old Testament that has frogs making big problems for humans (Exod 8:1-15).

4. Read or listen to Rev 16:13-14. Notice three frogs. Notice three hosts of the frogs, the dragon, the beast, and the false prophet. Compare the three animals in Rev 12-13: dragon, beast, and second beast, all focused on worshiping the dragon. Compare Rev 14:8 and 16:19 to discuss how Babylon, which is fallen, is made up of three parts.

5. Read or listen to Rev 16:13-14. These unclean spirits of the devils can work miracles. Compare Rev 13:14 to discover who worked miracles previously and for what purpose. Discuss what is the purpose of the miracles in Rev 16:13-14. Remind yourself, who has power over the devils?

Prayer Prompt: What means the most to you out of today's reading of Rev 16:13-14? What will you do about it now?

REV 16:15

1. Have you ever been robbed, or had someone break into your place or things? Tell about it and listen to others tell.

2. Read or listen to Rev 16:15. Compare Rev 3:11 and John 14:1-3, two other promises of Jesus's return. Notice in the contexts, what is or should be the reaction of people. Compare Rev 1:7 and Matt 24:27 to discover and discuss what Jesus's coming will be like.

3. Read or listen to Rev 16:15. Compare Rev 3:3 and Matt 24:42-44 to understand the reference to a thief. In what ways is Jesus's coming like and unlike the coming of a thief? Consider also John 10:1-10 for contrast in intent between Jesus and a thief.

4. Read or listen to Rev 16:15. Jesus said, keep your clothes, hang onto what you have (Rev 3:11). Research these garments in other parts of Revelation, color, material, how washed, and what they represent (Rev 3:4–5, 15–18; 6:11; 7:13–14; 19:7–8). Discuss.

5. Read or listen to Rev 16:15. What other characteristics go with nakedness in Rev 3:15–18? Will people buy clothes if they do not think they need them? Will people hang onto their clothes if they do not think they need them? How can we come to an awareness of our nakedness apart from Jesus?

Prayer Prompt: What means the most to you out of today's reading of Rev 16:15? What will you do about it now?

REV 16:16

1. At age nine, what kinds of things did you look forward to with happy anticipation? Tell and listen and discuss.

2. Read or listen to Rev 16:12–16. Verse 15, which shows Jesus's coming to be soon but not yet, interrupts the sixth plague call to Armageddon, the battle of the great day of the Lord. Research and compare other instances of the great day of the Lord (Joel 1:15; 2:1, 11, 31; 3:14; Amos 5:18–20; Obad 1:15; Zeph 1:7, 14; 14:1; Mal 4:5).

3. Read or listen to Rev 16:12–16. The kings of the east would be bringing deliverance. Retell some other instances of "east"(Isa 41:2; Ezek 42:1–4; Dan 11:44; Zech 14:4; Matt 24:27; Rev 7:2.)

4. Read or listen to Rev 16:12–16 with Isa 8:19–20 (compare Lev 19:31; 20:6; Deut 11:9–14). Discuss why God has such a warning against seeking communication with the spirits of the dead. Retell the story of Saul in his adventure with evil spirits (1 Sam 28; 1 Chr 10:13–14).

5. Read or listen to Rev 16:12–16. Armageddon, literally "Mountain of Megiddo," would bring to mind both a mountain and a valley. The mountain, Mount Carmel, was the location of God's showdown (1 Kgs 18), the valley was a site of many battles (Deborah, Judg 5:19–20; Jehu, 2 Kgs 9:22–27; Pharoah-Neco, 2 Kgs 23:29–30). Imagine and discuss: What might an all-out war between evil spirits and God look like?

Prayer Prompt: What means the most to you out of today's reading of Rev 16:12–16? What will you do about it now?

REV 16:17-21

1. Name and describe in your group some emotions you have felt on hearing a knock at your door or a ringing of the doorbell.

2. Read or listen to Rev 16:17-21, the seventh plague. First, please review all of the seventh, out of seven, increments so far in Revelation (Rev 11:15-19; 8:1; 3:14-22). Tell where you find Jesus in these vignettes, and how you feel about him here.

3. Read or listen to Rev 16:17-21. In the sixth increments, Jesus says, "I come quickly" (Rev 3:11 KJV; also Rev 16:15); now in the seventh increment comes the pronouncement, "It is done" (Rev 16:17 KJV). Compare Jesus's proclamation from the cross, "It is finished" (John 19:30 KJV). What do you think is finished or done in each of these statements?

4. Read or listen to Rev 16:17-21. Rev 16:19 is the last mention of the beasts until Rev 19:19-20, where they are conquered and destroyed during the Battle or Armageddon. Comparing Rev 16:11, 19 with Rev 19:19-20, what can you suggest about the three parts of Babylon?

5. Read or listen to Rev 16:17-21. Study Rev 16:5-6 and 17:6 to discover how it might be fair for God to release these pains on the earth. Read Rev 16:11, 21 to see how some people react to the "wrath" of God. Read Exod 34:6-7; Mic 6:8; and Rom 12:19 and discuss possible interactions between justice and mercy in God, and what is expected of humans.

Prayer Prompt: What means the most to you out of today's reading of Rev 16:17-21? What will you do about it now?

REV 17:1-7

1. Pick your favorite joke that turns on mystery, pun, or puzzle (only one, for now). Tell yours and listen to others tell theirs.

2. Read or listen to Rev 17:1-7. Who is the mystery that John is promised to see in this reading? Compare Rev 21:9-10 and discover whom John is told he will see in that reading. It will be interesting to notice comparisons and interactions between the Bride, the Lamb, and Babylon.

3. Read or listen to Rev 17:1-3. Create a picture in your mind of this woman. Discover two different things this reading says she sits on.

Put those two different things in your picture. Compare Rev 12:3, 9 and 13:1-2 with 17:1-3. List the similarities and differences between these animals.

4. Read or listen to Rev 17:2-6. Compare Rev 14:1 to discover who else has a name written in the forehead. Read Rev 6:9-10; 12:17; 16:6, and tell whose blood is in the cup she holds. What other illegal relationships does she have? What is blasphemy, according to Mark 2:5-7; 14:61-64?

5. Read or listen to Rev 17:7. Use your imagination to think about what to expect in the remainder of Rev 17. Talk together about what other mysteries or puzzles you would like to know about these things.

Prayer Prompt: What means the most to you out of today's reading of Rev 17:1-7? What will you do about it now?

REV 17:7-18

1. Think about the knock-knock jokes. Tell some and listen to some. Discuss what makes them work.

2. Read or listen to Rev 17:7-18. This continues the explanation given by the angel about the judgment of Babylon. Please circle in the reading every verb of being: is, are, was, were, will be. Then make a list of a few symbols with their definitions or equations to other symbols as discovered here.

3. Read or listen to Rev 17:8-11. Notice the lack of their names in the book of life, and their destination of destruction. Compare Rev 13:1, 8 to note that the animal on which Babylon rides is similar to the animal from the sea. Earlier we noticed the similarities between the ridden animal and the great red dragon (comparing Rev 17:3 with 12:3, 9). Can you posit a reason for all these similarities?

4. Read or listen to Rev 17:9-10. This portion is often called an "enigma" or "riddle." Think like a first-century Christian of Jewish heritage. The world-power nations in Jewish history were Egypt, Assyria, Babylon, Persia, Greece, and Rome. Yet to come was religious Rome and all the events since the Reformation and the French Revolution. Discuss.

5. Read or listen to Rev 17:7-18. Find symbolic meanings in the Scripture itself for "ten horns" and "waters." Please focus on what happens when these all make war with the Lamb in Rev 17:14, the next phase

of Armageddon. What do you think it means to be "called, and chosen, and faithful"?

Prayer Prompt: What means the most to you out of today's reading of Rev 17:7–18? What will you do about it now?

REV 18:1–24

1. When have you been the underdog? And when the upper dog? Tell your group about one of those times.
2. Read or listen to Rev 18:1–5. Recall from the Old Testament two stories about Babylon (Gen 11:1–9; Dan 4:29–37). What is the call of God to God's people regarding Babylon?
3. Read or listen to Rev 18:10–19. Find the three laments over Babylon beginning with the word, "Alas!" Who speaks them? What are their similarities and differences? Compare and contrast these with the laments in the seven seals (Rev 6:6, 10, 16). Discuss the need for lament when things are bad.
4. Read or listen to Rev 18. Please connect with your underdog experiences to read this. Babylon is the forces united against the underdog, the arrogance and coercion of consumerism, the reduction of all to monetization, the criminalization of being poor or homeless, the commandeering of language into lies, libel, inflation, entrapment, nonsense, and blasphemy; the relentless flow of noise in order to fatigue, benumb, and demoralize the public. You and I can read Revelation and come awake! Discuss.
5. Read or listen again to Rev 18:1–5. Read these verses aloud together maybe taking parts for dramatic reading. Discuss what is the solution for God's people in the face of church, corporation, and country who unite money, prestige, and force against making God first?

Prayer Prompt: What means the most to you out of today's reading of Rev 18? What will you do about it now?

REV 19:1–6

1. Tell the group about the first time you heard the word "Alleluia" or "Hallelujah"—describe setting and feelings.

2. Read or listen to Rev 19:1–6. Find, count, notice, all the "Alleluias" here. Compare them with "Alas" in Rev 18.

3. Read or listen to Rev 19:1–6 and 4–5. Find as many similar phrases and themes as you can and note the dissimilarities. Compare the judgment of Rev 6:10 and Rev 11:18 with that of Rev 19:2.

4. Read or listen to Rev 19:3. Have you ever heard anyone say that part of the eternal joy of the saints will be look out over hell to watch sinners burning in pain? That is not a picture to connect with a loving God. Then let us deconstruct that theory. (a) Neither God nor God's people ever take any pleasure in the death of anyone (Ezek 33:11; Luke 9:56). (b) Sinners die because they have chosen against life not because of the fire (Matt 25:41; Rev 20:15). (c) No one is burning in hell right now (John 5:28–29; 2 Pet 2:9). (d) No one will burn forever (Ps 37:10, 20; Mal 4:3). (e) In the Bible, there is "unquenchable fire," "everlasting punishment," "everlasting fire," "tormented forever." Consider these as explanation: Jer 17:27; Jude 1:7; 2 Pet 2:6; Jonah 1:17; 2:6; Deut 23:3.

5. Read or listen again to Rev 19:1–6. Find Jesus and something about the character of God and Jesus in this reading. Tell about it and listen to someone else tell about their findings.

Prayer Prompt: What means the most to you out of today's reading of Rev 19:1–6? What will you do about it now?

REV 19:6–10

1. What do you like most about weddings. Tell someone and listen to others tell.

2. Read or listen to Rev 19:6–10. Review and discuss who is telling the story of Revelation, and to whom. See Rev 1:1–2; 22:6–9.

3. Read or listen to Rev 19:6–10. Find connections that will help explain the marriage supper, and discuss them. See Matt 22:1–14; Luke 14:15; Rev 21:9–10.

4. Read or listen to Rev 19:1–6. Review the other instances of fine or white linen. Discuss how this reading helps or hinders the understanding of the others (Rev 3:4–5, 18; 4:4; 6:11; 7:13–14; 19:14). Also compare the persons dressed in linen (Rev 18:12, 16; 19:14). Describe the bride as contrasted with Babylon.

5. Read or listen again to Rev 19:9–10. Compare and contrast Rev 22:6–9. What is the testimony of Jesus (compare 1 Cor 12:7–11)? What does the testimony of Jesus do for humans (Rev 1:9; 6:9; 12:11, 17)? Discuss what you will do to have and give the testimony of Jesus more often.

Prayer Prompt: What means the most to you out of today's reading of Rev 19:6–10? What will you do about it now?

REV 19:11–16

1. Describe in your group some of what you see when you try to imagine God or Jesus. How has reading the book of Revelation colored or enhanced your imagination in this?

2. Read or listen to Rev 19:11–16. Compare and contrast the previous descriptions of Jesus in Rev 1:12–16; 5:6.

3. Read or listen to Rev 19:11–16. Notice the emphasis on names, and list all the names for Jesus given here. Compare Rev 3:14; John 1:1, 14; Dan 2:47. Which name for Jesus means the most to you right now?

4. Read or listen to Rev 19:11–16. Who else dipped clothes in blood (Rev 7:14; 12:11)? Find and contrast three persons or groups dressed in fine linen (Rev 18:12, 16; 19:8, 14). Which group would you choose?

5. Read or listen again to Rev 19:11–16. Find the sharp sword in Rev 1:16; 2:12, 16; 13:10; 19:15, and also in Eph 6:17 and Heb 4:12. Do you remember other Bible claims for the joy and goodness of the Bible? Why do you think it is or is not logically sound to believe the Bible's claims for itself?

Prayer Prompt: What means the most to you out of today's reading of Rev 19:11–16? What will you do about it now?

REV 19:17–21

1. Describe the most extravagant feast you have attended.

2. Read or listen to Rev 19:17–21. Please take a few minutes to read these additional sections before and after the section for today: Rev 16:13, 19; 17:16–17; 18:9; 19:9, 17–21; 20:9–10; 21:9–10. Read them several times in varying voices and settings. Read the entire context (Rev 16–21) if you have time. Read and follow each entity, devil, beast,

false prophet, kings of the earth, remnant. Allow yourself and others to have the sadness for God's creation and created beings who refuse him.

3. Read or listen to Rev 19:17-21. We are beginning to approach the one thousand years that takes up most of Rev 20. From Scripture only, not from what you have heard, try to put together "Before," "During," and "After" lists for the one thousand years.

4. Read or listen to Rev 19:17-21. Name and describe the two feasts or "suppers" (Rev 19:9, 17).

5. Read or listen again to Rev 19:17-21. Try to differentiate who goes into the fire and who goes under the sword. Discuss, remembering that the sword is the Word of God (Eph 6:17; Heb 4:12; Ps 1; 19; 119), and our God is a consuming fire (Heb 12:29).

Prayer Prompt: What means the most to you out of today's reading of Rev 19:17-21? What will you do about it now?

REV 20:1-15

1. Make a spread sheet or mural with three columns, headed: "Before," "During," and "After." Add the two events from Rev 19 in the "Before" column:

   - 19:11—Jesus comes from heaven.
   - 19:21—Remnant of God-resistors die by the sword.

2. Read or listen to Rev 20:1-15, noting all the mentions of one thousand years. Now enter on your spreadsheet these events in the columns indicated, as related to the one thousand years.

   - 20:2—Satan bound—"Before"
   - 20:2—Satan stays bound—"During"
   - 20:3, 7—Satan loosed—"After"
   - 20:4, 6—God's witnesses, the saints, are with Jesus—"During"
   - 20:5—First resurrection (witnesses, saints)—"Before"
   - 20:5—Second resurrection (rest of the dead, resistors)—"After"

3. Read or listen to Rev 20:9–21:2. Then place these additional events in the "After" column:

- 20:6—God's witnesses, the saints, are in the city.
- 20:7-9—Satan incites war against the city of the saints.
- 20:9—God-resistors are devoured by fire.
- 20:10—Satan is sent into the fire.
- 20:14-15—Second death of God-resistors.
- 21:2—Holy city descends from heaven.

4. Read again Rev 20:10, 14-15. Who goes into the fire?
5. Read or listen again to Rev 20:1-15. Ponder your spreadsheet and follow together the fortunes around the one thousand years of these: witnesses or saints, God-resistors, Satan, earth itself.

Prayer Prompt: What means the most to you out of today's reading of Rev 20:1-15? What will you do about it now?

REV 20:11-15

1. When was the last time you did jumping jacks for exercise? Tell how it went for you.
2. Read or listen to Rev 20:11-15. Please notice several items here: the throne, the face, the books, opened, book of life, judged. Note their context, content, colors, powers, etc.
3. Read or listen to Rev 20:11-15. Find some of the items listed above in Rev 13:8 and 4:1—5:14. Compare and contrast these items found at Revelation's beginning (Rev 4-5), middle (Rev 13), and end (Rev 20) of Revelation.
4. Read again Rev 20:11-15. Then read Esth 6:1-3. Scan the story of Esther to discover the place in the plot where the book was opened. What was the king's concern after hearing the book read?
5. Read or listen again to Rev 20:11-15. Now read and compare Dan 7:9-14, regarding the same items already highlighted. This is a hint that we will study Daniel after Revelation. They are like the two halves of a jumping jack child, mirror images of one another, fascinating

for knowing God. Bonus: Find and ponder these same items in Matt 25:31–40.

Prayer Prompt: What means the most to you out of today's reading of Rev 20:11–15? What will you do about it now?

REV 21:1

1. Research how many satellites are in orbit. Tell about them.
2. Read or listen to Rev 21:1—22:5. Let your thoughts and feelings get lost in the sounds of these words, and the images they let you imagine. Read the passage aloud and together.
3. Read or listen to Rev 21:1. From where did the first heaven and earth come (Gen 1:1–2)? Where have they gone by this point in Revelation (Rev 20:11; Dan 2:35)? What is left of them (2 Pet 3:10–13; Isa 65:17)?
4. Read or listen again to Rev 21:1. Which of these heavens do you think is included in this clean-up? Sky, the heaven where the birds fly (Gen 1:6–8, 20)? Space, the heaven where the stars and planets orbit (Gen 1:14–19; Ps 147:4)? Or God's home, the high and holy place (Isa 57:15; 1 Kgs 8:27–49; Isa 66:1)? Are you willing to be ready for the cleanup?
5. Read or listen again to Rev 21:1. Make a list of who and what get to be no more (Rev 19:20; 20:10, 13; 21:1, 4; 22:5; 18:21). What had Babylon done on the sea (Rev 18:17–19)? Earlier an entire mountain was thrown into the sea and only affected a third of the sea (Rev 8:8). Here Rev 21:1 pictures a time when a mountain will fill the whole earth, and there will be no more sea, no more oppressions making someone else rich. Compare and discuss Dan 2:35.

Prayer Prompt: What means the most to you out of today's reading of Rev 21:1? What will you do about it now?

REV 21:2–4

1. Tell your group about someone or something that wants to be with you much of the time, and tell how you feel about it.
2. Read or listen to Rev 21:2–4. Compare Rev 21:2 with 19:7–8 to think and talk about who is husband and who is bride. When do you think is the wedding?

3. Read or listen to Rev 21:2–4. Compare Rev 21:2 to 3:12. Read Rev 3:7–13 to discover what were the issues in the church to which this promise was made.

4. Read or listen again to Rev 21:2–4. Compare Exod 25:8 to discover and discuss what is the purpose of the Old Testament tabernacle (sanctuary). Read Lev 23:34–43 and describe together a feast that was made to commemorate and preview this time when God would dwell with God's people.

5. Read or listen again to Rev 21:2–4. List the things that will be no more when God actually dwells with God's people. Choose one thing in this reading that makes you happy to think about its absence. Tell your group about it with imaginative description and tell why its absence makes you happy.

Prayer Prompt: What means the most to you out of today's reading of Rev 21:2–4? What will you do about it now?

REV 21:5–8

1. Tell about a time when someone was loyal and honest to you even if it cost time, courage, clear thinking, or something else.

2. Read or listen to Rev 21:5–8. These are three sayings by the One who sat on the throne, the last of the three being the longest. Notice the remarkable structure of this book of Revelation, flagged right here. Find the references to something from the first of the book (Rev 1:8; 2:7, 11, 17, 26; 3:5, 12, 21; notice also Rev 12:11). Discuss the meaning of this repetition.

3. Read or listen to Rev 21:5–8. Find the other two mentions of the water of life (Rev 7:17; 22:17) and sit with the images to absorb them and discuss your feelings. Now read John 4:1–15; 7:37–39. Do you think water is a good metaphor for the Holy Spirit?

4. Read or listen again to Rev 21:5–8. According to John 1:12, how does one become a son of God? Is this related to Rev 21:7? If so, discuss how.

5. Read or listen again to Rev 21:5–8. In your next reading of Rev 21–22, find the three lists like the one in Rev 21:8. Then discover the one item included in all three lists. Look in Rev 3:5; 19:11; and 22:6 to discover why this characteristic is most excluded from the new world.

Prayer Prompt: What means the most to you out of today's reading of Rev 21:5-8? What will you do about it now?

REV 21:9-22

1. Tell about an experience of finding out that something is much bigger than you expected it to be.
2. Read or listen to Rev 21:9-22. For the backstory on Jerusalem, look for Mount Moriah in Gen 22; 1 Chr 21; and 2 Chr 3-4. What might Abraham and David have to say about the foundations of Jerusalem?
3. Read or listen to Rev 21:9-22. Careful measurements and a cubicle structure given to Moses on the mountain had to do with the first tent-temple the Israelites made for God (Exod 24-40; Heb 8:5). Careful measurements, a mountain, and a wall had to do with what Ezekiel saw as a new temple for God (Ezek 40-48). Why such careful measurements? Why would this city be likened to the temple?
4. Read or listen again to Rev 21:9-22. Find the twelve jewels named for the twelve tribes of Israel on the priests' breastplate in Exod 28:17-21, 29-30. Compare this to the jewels and their names in the foundation in Rev 21 (see also Eph 2:19-21). Where are the tribes' names in Rev 21?
5. Read or listen again to Rev 21:22. The city here is measured and cubical like a temple. John says he saw no temple in all the city. What reason does he give? Next time you feel like you cannot see God or feel God near, remind yourself to look a little bigger. Reminds me of "He is not here; He is risen" (Matt 28:6).

Prayer Prompt: What means the most to you out of today's reading of Rev 21:9-22? What will you do about it now?

REV 21:22-27

1. Where were the light switches in your home growing up? How old were you when you were allowed to turn them on and off?
2. Read or listen to Rev 21:22-27. First, notice the things specifically stated as not present here. And tell what the Scripture gives as the reason for their absence.

3. Read or listen to Rev 21:22–27. Who or what is the source of light for this city? Who walks in that light? Who brings their praises into it?

4. Read or listen again to Rev 21:25. Compare Matt 16:18. Imagine in pictures a war between the gates of this city and the gates of hell. Which are shut and which are open? Which are aggressive? Which are more inviting? Compare Rev 22:14 to discover and discuss who has the right to go into the gates of this city.

5. Read or listen again to Rev 21:27. It is not the right of human judgment to decide which is dirty, detestable, or deceitful and thereby excluded from this city. It is the Lamb's book of life that determines who goes in. How do you think a person's name gets into the Lamb's book of life (John 3:16)? How might a person's name get taken out of the book of life (Rev 3:5; Exod 32:31–33)? How seriously do you think God takes the books (Rev 20:12; Daniel 7:10)?

Prayer Prompt: What means the most to you out of today's reading of Rev 21:22–27? What will you do about it now?

REV 22:1–2

1. Name three things you have to have in order to live. Discuss.

2. Read or listen to Rev 22:1–2. Find the mentions of "life" in this reading. Draw or describe the pictures related to life that you see in your imagination as you read these verses.

3. Read or listen to Rev 22:1–2. Compare Ezek 47:1, 12, and find similarities and differences in the sources and descriptions of the river and the tree.

4. Read or listen again to Rev 22:1–2. Compare Rev 2:7, and consider what might be the benefits of starting over in the reading of Revelation to catch all these early references to the end parts. Read Gen 2:9–10 to discover the origins of this tree and river. Draw, paint, poeticize, dance, or sing these beginnings.

5. Read or listen again to Rev 22:1–2. Describe the fruit of the tree of life. Describe the purpose of the leaves of the tree of life. Look at Matt 4:23; 9:35, and discover what was Jesus's work on earth. Brainstorm together about how each one can contribute to healing in other persons.

Prayer Prompt: What means the most to you out of today's reading of Rev 22:1–2? What will you do about it now?

REV 22:3–5

1. Tell of a childhood imagination of yours around being king or queen, prince or princess.
2. Read or listen to Rev 22:3–5. Compare Gen 3:14–19; Nah 1:9; and Rev 7:15–17. Discuss what curse is meant, and how far-reaching its results. What will change when this curse is no more? Tell what you like most about life without curse.
3. Read or listen to Rev 22:3–5. Review and retell the story of Moses regarding God's face (Exod 33:9—34:6; Num 12:6–8). Discuss the difference between seeing or not seeing a person's face. (You might ponder and mention the power Facebook gleans from that difference.)
4. Read or listen again to Rev 22:3–5. Review the mentions in Revelation of something written in the forehead (Rev 3:12; 7:3; 13:16; 14:1; 20:4). Can you decide and testify right now what you want written in your forehead?
5. Read or listen again to Rev 22:3–5. Compare Rev 20:4 and notice the difference between "a thousand years" and "for ever and ever" as the length of time they will reign. What other things are different about reigning in these two different settings? Review Rev 1:5–6, and see what Paul makes of the idea in 1 Cor 6:1–3. How will you live today in light of the fact that you will forever sit as king or queen?

Prayer Prompt: What means the most to you out of today's reading of Rev 22:3–5? What will you do about it now?

REV 22:6–10

1. Talk and listen to each other tell how easy or hard it is to write an "X" in cursive lower case or upper case.
2. Read or listen to Rev 22:6–10. These verses begin the epilogue of the book of Revelation. Other mentions of "faithful and true" are in Rev 19:9; 3:14; 1:5. Other mentions of the angel and why he came are in Rev 4:1; 1:1; as well as in Dan 2:28–29. Read, compare, discuss.

INVITATIONS TO DISCUSSION 149

3. Read or listen to Rev 22:7. Other mentions of the quick return of Jesus are in Rev 3:11; 1:7. Another mention of the blessing for reading this book is in Rev 1:3. What might be the function, for the reader, of these repetitive mentions at the beginning and end of the book of Revelation?

4. Read or listen to Rev 22:8–9. Compare Rev 19:10 and Rev 14:6–12. Why does the angel refuse to let John worship him?

5. Read or listen to Rev 22:10. Compare the sealed book in Rev 5:1–5 and the open book in Rev 10:2. Compare also the shut and sealed books in Dan 8:26; 12:4, 9. What did Jesus say about understanding the book of Daniel (Matt 24:15)?

Prayer Prompt: What means the most to you out of today's reading of Rev 22:6–10? What will you do about it now?

REV 22:11-15

1. Have you ever served on a jury? Review together the various parts and participants in a trial in the American justice system.

2. Read or listen to Rev 22:11–15. This section begins with a statement of judgment finished. That is, a little while before Jesus comes, the choices of people have been made and settled forever, whether for injustice and filth or for justice and holiness. Tell your group of the feelings this thought arouses.

3. Read or listen to Rev 22:12–13. Look all around in Rev 22 for seven instances of this word "Come." Ponder and discuss how the word is used, who is speaking, and why there are seven instances. Find similarities also in Rev 1 and discuss why this word appears in both places.

4. Read or listen to Rev 22:14–15. See if you can match the negative words (Rev 22:15) with the commandments (Exod 20:1–17). Note: "Dogs" was used as a demeaning name for anyone who did not follow the commandments (Matt 15:26–27; 2 Pet 2:21–22). According to Rev 22:14, what is the way to the justice and holiness mentioned in Rev 22:11?

5. Read or listen to Rev 22:11–15. Consider and discuss, How many parts are there to thorough judgment and justice? Which parts are done before Jesus comes? Which parts are done at Jesus's coming? Pray the

Lord's Prayer, the Our Father, together, noticing the request, "Thy kingdom come" (Matt 6:10).

Prayer Prompt: What means the most to you out of today's reading of Rev 22:11–15? What will you do about it now?

REV 22:16-19

1. Tell someone who will listen about your experiences in reading the book of Revelation.
2. Read or listen to Rev 22:16–19. About the angel who testifies (Rev 22:16, 20), compare Rev 1:1–2. What incentive do you find in discovering the end at the beginning in the book of Revelation? For "Root of David," compare Rev 5:5, and for the "morning star," compare Rev 2:28. Notice and discuss how the contexts are similar or different.
3. Read or listen to Rev 22:17. Compare John 4:1–42; 7:37–39. Please help each other take this in: the Holy Spirit can be in you bubbling up into understanding as you read the word of God.
4. Read or listen to Rev 22:18–19. Note the dire consequences of tampering with the words of God. For example, if a person tampers, even subconsciously, with the internal statement of first audience or first hearers of these words, then there are pitfalls on both sides of theological thought: either we make the writing into fiction created for some other purpose than internally stated, or we make the writing into a dogmatic tool for our own purposes. Let us hear through the ears of the internally identified first audience, as hearing testimony of their experience.
5. Read or listen to Rev 22:18–19. Compare the curses here with the blessing in Rev 1:3. Which will you choose today?

Prayer Prompt: What means the most to you out of today's reading of Rev 22:16–19? What will you do about it now?

REV 22:20-21

1. Tell and listen as others tell what it feels like to finish a course. Talk about coming to the end of the book of Revelation.

2. Read or listen to Rev 22:20–21. Discuss the other mentions of "come" in this epilogue (Rev 22:7, 12, 17). Which of these are Jesus's announcement, which are response to that announcement, and which are invitation to new participation? List all the parties who agree in the desire for Jesus to come.

3. Read or listen to Rev 22:20–21. Compare the other mention of Jesus's coming in Rev 1:7. What can you glean here about how Jesus will come again? What information can you add to your picture from Rev 2:5, 16, 25; 3:3, 11, 20; 16:15?

4. Read or listen to Rev 22:20–21. How quick is quickly? It has been two thousand years. The small church in Thessalonica was worried about the delay. Read 1 Thess 4:13–18; 5:1–6; and 2 Thess 2:1–10, to hear Paul's heart and instruction regarding the delay.

5. Read or listen to Rev 22:20–21. What does the "grace of our Lord Jesus Christ" in benediction mean to you? Compare Rev 1:4–5 and tell who sends this grace. Discuss.

Prayer Prompt: What means the most to you out of today's reading of Rev 22:20–21? What will you do about it now?

DAN 1:1–16

1. Tell someone who will listen something about your acquaintance with the book of Daniel in the Old Testament.

2. Read or listen to Dan 1:1–16. Compare 2 Kings 24:1 and 2 Chr 36:6 to get the back story. Discuss what it must mean to have your homeland destroyed by war and all familiar customs banned, then to be taken as aliens to a new land.

3. Read or listen to Dan 1:1–7. Compare Rev 1:9 to discuss the historical similarities and differences in the experiences of Daniel in Babylon and John on Patmos.

4. Read or listen to Dan 1:4–16. Notice the imposition of new names, new language, new learning, and new food. Describe the test and its results. For how many days was this test? Compare Rev 2:10, and discuss the similarities and differences in the effects of these identical time periods. List other similarities you discover between Dan 1 and Rev 1–3.

5. Read or listen to Dan 1:9, 15. How were Daniel and his friends blessed in this encounter? How was John blessed on Patmos (Rev 1:10-20)? How can you and I be blessed in the midst of our encounters with trouble?

Prayer Prompt: What means the most to you out of today's reading of Dan 1:1-16? What will you do about it now?

DAN 1:17-21

1. Discuss with your group, How important are grades to you?
2. Read or listen to Dan 1:17-21. Compare Dan 12:3-4, 8, 10, and Rev 13:8. Discuss: How important do you think understanding is in the two books, Daniel and Revelation?
3. Read or listen to Dan 1:17-21. Compare Ps 119:97-104 and Prov 4:7. Though we do not know the date of either this psalm or this proverb, what might one deduce from the prevalence in Israel of prayers to God for understanding?
4. Read or listen to Dan 1:17-21. Compare Joel 2:27-19 and Acts 2:15-18. Young men and women seeing visions and dreaming dreams was associated with the day of the Lord, the coming of the Messiah. How might visions and dreams prepare the world for the Messiah?
5. Read or listen to Dan 1:17-21. Read also Dan 9:25-26 and realize that Daniel was a prophet of the Messiah. Talk and listen to each other about some of the benefits that Jesus's being the Messiah offers you and your family.

Prayer Prompt: What means the most to you out of today's reading of Dan 1:17-21? What will you do about it now?

DAN 2

1. Tell in your group of a dream you have had that you thought meant something.
2. Read or listen to Dan 2. First, let us focus on the story surrounding the dream. Can you discover the timing of this story in comparison to the story of Dan 1? What problem was in the King's chambers? How did Daniel and his friends learn of the problem (Dan 2:13)?

INVITATIONS TO DISCUSSION   153

3. Read or listen to Dan 2:13–25. List in order the steps Daniel took in the face of this emergency. Ponder and discuss the contents of Daniel's two prayers, the petition and the praise.

4. Read or listen to Dan 2:31–45. Now let us focus on the dream and its meaning. Make seven sections going down your page. Label them 1) gold, 2) silver, 3) brass, 4) iron, 5) iron and clay, 6) mixed and mingled but not united, 7) God's kingdom. Then note everything you can find pertaining to each section.

5. Read or listen to Dan 2:26–30 and 46–49. Remember Dan 1:17 where it was noted that Daniel had special understanding. From where did Daniel affirm that this special understanding came? Compare Dan 2:28 with Rev 1:19 to discover the theme of both books. What does this mean to you?

Prayer Prompt: What means the most to you out of today's reading of Dan 2? What will you do about it now?

DAN 2:19–47

1. If anyone in the group has done geocaching, tell and listen about it. Or tell about a time you looked for something hidden.

2. Read or listen to Dan 2:19–47. Count how many times "reveal" and its derivatives are used. "Revealing" is the English translation of "Apocalypse," which is the word in the Greek translations of this passage. In what ways does this king's dream, as revealed to Daniel, foreshadow the book of Revelation, the Apocalypse, in the New Testament?

3. Read or listen to Dan 10:1. Something was revealed ("apocalypse") to Daniel and he understood it. We are not told what it was except that it involved a long time. Read the rest of Dan 10 and make a list of descriptions of Daniel's reactions in both his mourning and the subsequent events.

4. Read or listen to Dan 2:19–47. What was revealed ("apocalypse") and why was that important? Who got the credit? Do you think it could be said that this story is an apocalypse of God, a revealing of God' glory and power?

5. Read or listen to Dan 2:19–47. From whatever amount you have read in the book of Revelation, how would you describe the ways in which

that book is "the Revelation of Jesus Christ," as its apocalyptic heading asserts?

Prayer Prompt: What means the most to you out of today's reading of Dan 2:19–47? What will you do about it now?

DAN 3

1. Tell six specific things you do that are related to your life dream. Tell how they are related to what you envision for yourself.
2. Read or listen to Dan 3. First, let us research the local context. Where is gold last seen in Daniel? Discuss what might this king's action have had to do with the king's dream in Dan 2. Though we do not know much about the plain of Dura, we do know the province of Babylon where they gathered was the land of Shinar (Dan 1:2), and Shinar had history as a place of building (Gen 11:1–4). Compare and discuss the story of Babel with this story of Babylon.
3. Read or listen to Dan 3:1, 4, 10, 24–25. Now let us notice the literary connections. Compare Rev 13:15–18; 14:6–12; 4:5; 5:6, the numbers, the decrees, the fire, and Jesus.
4. Read or listen to Dan 3. Tell, draw, dance, or dramatize the story. Where would you decide are the apex and climax of the story? The high point and the main point?
5. Read or listen to Dan 3:17–18. Research, find, and tell a story of someone who believed and trusted in God through very great trouble, despite a grim outlook. What could you do today to increase your belief and trust in God?

Prayer Prompt: What means the most to you out of today's reading of Dan 3? What will you do about it now?

DAN 3:1-18

1. How many icons do you have at your house? How many do you see in your group's meeting place? How many can you think of in society? Tell of your favorite icon.
2. Read or listen to Dan 3:1–18. "Icon" is a word brought over from the Greek, meaning, "statue" or "image." It can be two- or three-dimensional.

INVITATIONS TO DISCUSSION   155

It can be a poor or fine representation. It can be cheap or expensive. "Idol" is another word brought over from the Greek, meaning, "statue" or "image." Discuss the different connotations which group members attach to these words.

3. Read or listen to Dan 3:1–18 with Rev 13:12–17. Compare and contrast the two stories and their images. Who made the images? Who required their worship? What was the means of killing? Who was delivered, by whom?

4. Read or listen to Dan 3:1–18 with 1 Cor 8:1–13; 10:1–33. It is long reading yet instructive from Paul about eating food that had been offered to "idols." Share with the group what stands out to you from this reading.

5. Read or listen to Dan 3:1–18 with Rev 2:12–29. Notice the words "stumbling block" and "seduce." How do these words color the acts of eating and sex? Why do you think these two actions, eating food sacrificed to idols and fornication, would be singled out as most dangerous and hated by Jesus?

Prayer Prompt: What means the most to you out of today's reading of Dan 3:1–18? What will you do about it now?

DAN 4

1. Tell someone who will listen what you like most about this season of the year. What will you do to stay more connected with nature?

2. Read or listen to Dan 4. Who is speaking? To whom? Why do you think a non-Israelite tyrant of a king got to write a portion of our Bible?

3. Read or listen to Dan 4 with Rev 6–7. Consider especially Dan 4:34–37 and Rev 7:12–17, looking for similar words, phrases, or scenes. The point is the worship and service of God as ultimate king. The miracle is the preservation of the kingdom. The means is the banding of a tree and or the sealing of the saints. Discuss similarities and differences.

4. Read or listen to Dan 4. Tell, draw, dance, or dramatize the story. Compare Dan 4:30–31 with Rev 14:8. Tell what you think is the problem with Babylon.

5. Read or listen to Dan 4:34–37. Find some words that assert God's authority as king. Find other words that assert human nothingness. Find yet other words that assert human discovery and excellence. Discuss

how these three items fit in your life, God's authority, human nothingness or helplessness, and human excellence.

Prayer Prompt: What means the most to you out of today's reading of Dan 4? What will you do about it now?

DAN 5

1. Are your grandchildren doing what you wish they were? Are you doing what your grandparents wished for you? Tell someone who will listen to you.
2. Read or listen to Dan 5. Belshazzar was Nebuchadnezzar's grandson. Since Belshazzar's father Nabunidus did not like to rule, he put the kingdom in the hands of his son. Belteshazzar was the name given to Daniel by Nebuchadnezzar. Discuss why you think Daniel was missing from the party at first.
3. Read or listen to Dan 5 with Rev 8–11. Consider especially Dan 5:1–4, 26 with Rev 9:20; 10:7; and 11:10, looking for similar words, phrases, or scenes. The point in both books is that there is a last night for oppressors.
4. Read or listen to Dan 5. Re-tell, draw, dance, or dramatize the story. Compare Dan 5:18–23 with Rev 14:8. Tell what you think is the problem with Babylon.
5. Read or listen to Dan 5:18–23 with Dan 4:34–37. Describe and discuss what it was that Belshazzar did not learn from his grandfather Nebuchadnezzar. Scholars think the queen in Dan 5:10 is the queen-mother, Nebuchadnezzar's wife, Belshazzar's grandmother. What are you learning from your grandparents about following God?

Prayer Prompt: What means the most to you out of today's reading of Dan 5? What will you do about it now?

DAN 6

1. Have you ever been bullied because you were kind to someone or because you did good work? Tell your group what happened.
2. Read or listen to Dan 6. Review Dan 5 to know how Darius came to be the new management. Compare Dan 6:3–4 with Rev 14:5. Compare

INVITATIONS TO DISCUSSION 157

the decree in Dan 6:7–13 with decrees in Dan 3:8–12 and Rev 13:15. Review Dan 4:24–25, and tell each other whose decrees are stronger.

3. Read or listen to Dan 6 with 1 Pet 5:8 and Rev 12. Who is the lion-dragon now? How does he show himself in our lives and society? What did the angel do to the lions for Daniel?

4. Read or listen to Dan 6. Who slept well? Who did not sleep well? How do you think the bullies slept? To whom did both Daniel and the king give credit for a safe night (Dan 6:20–21)? The narrator also gives credit, or a reason. What is it (Dan 6:23)?

5. Read or listen to Dan 6:25–28. Read aloud together the words of the proclamation or decree that Darius finally made. Listen to the sound of your voices blending. How effective is a human decree for these things? What will you do today that will go beyond the making of a decree?

Prayer Prompt: What means the most to you out of today's reading of Dan 6? What will you do about it now?

DAN 6:16–25

1. "Sticks and stones may break my bones, but words can never hurt me." When have you tried to tell yourself or someone else that this saying is true? When have you wanted to scream that it is not true?

2. Read or listen to Dan 6:16–25. How many times is the word "mouth" or "mouths" used in this reading? Compare and count the number of times it appears in Dan 7:5–20. Find the lies and flatteries in Dan 11:21–34. Tell whether or not, and why, you think these are helpful or hurtful uses of the mouth.

3. Read or listen to Dan 6:16–25. Compare Dan 7:25 with Rev 13:2–6 in terms of the use of the mouth. Compare also Rev 9:17–19; 12:15–16. Notice how large an impact a mouth can have. Share any experiences you wish to, of being hurt by what came out of someone's mouth.

4. Read or listen to Dan 6:16–25. Compare Dan 4:31, and notice that while the words of pride were still in his mouth there came a voice from heaven. How do you react to the fact that there is another voice in the universe besides the hurtful ones? Would you like Jesus to send his angels to shut the lion's mouths?

5. Read or listen to Dan 6:16–25. Compare Rev 1:16; 2:12, 16. What is it that comes out of Jesus's mouth? Comparing Heb 4:12 could let us see this that is coming out of Jesus's mouth as his words, or Scripture, or even testimony, witness, or prophecy. What does he do with it?

Prayer Prompt: What means the most to you out of today's reading of Dan 6:16–25? What will you do about it now?

DAN 7:1-15

1. How do you tell whether or not a dream of yours has meaning for your life? Discuss with your group using dreams as symbols or for life improvement or advancement.

2. Read or listen to Dan 7:1–15. Briefly review and tell the story of Belshazzar from Dan 5, so you will know the setting in which Daniel saw and wrote this dream. Why do you think he mentioned that he told the "whole matter"?

3. Read or listen to Dan 7:1–15. Re-tell or draw the dream step by step. Do not try to make meaning of each picture or scene. Just immerse and soak in the dream itself. After doing this well, tell how you feel having waked up.

4. Read or listen to Dan 7:1–15. Notice and discuss these connections to Revelation: Lion, Bear, Leopard animals from the sea (Rev 13:1–2); Books (Rev 13:8); God's Judgment (Rev 14:7). What do you think it means that the strongest connection between Daniel and Revelation lies at the center of each book?

5. Read or listen to Dan 7:1–15. Locate the "Ancient of Days" and the "Son of Man" in the scene. What is the role of each? What happened to the animals in the dream? (Compare Rev 19:19–20 for the animals.) (Compare Mark 2:10, 28 for what authority the "Son of Man" has.)

Prayer Prompt: What means the most to you out of today's reading of Dan 7:1–15? What will you do about it now?

DAN 7:15-28

1. Have you ever been in a conversation so lively that, afterward, you could not remember which idea came from whom? Tell.

2. Read or listen to Dan 7:15–28. Section this reading according to who is speaking, and notice Daniel's increasing concern. Discuss which part of the dream concerned Daniel the most and what new information Daniel added to the account in the retelling (Dan 7:19–22).

3. Read or listen to Dan 7:15–28. Sort and evaluate the interpretations given by the "one who stood by" (Dan 7:17–18; 23–27). Why do you think the explainer would wait for Daniel to ask and describe before going into more in-depth interpretation?

4. Read or listen to Dan 7:15–28. Compare Dan 7:21 with Rev 12:17 to learn who makes war with the saints. Compare Dan 7:25 with Rev 12:17 to learn what happens to God's laws in each instance. Compare Dan 7:25 with Rev 12:14 to notice identical descriptions of time. Consider again what the strong connections between Dan 7 and Rev 12–14 might mean.

5. Read or listen to Dan 7:15–28. Discuss the difference between who got the kingdom in Daniel's dream (Dan 7:13–14) and who gets the kingdom in the explainer's interpretation (Dan 7:27). Compare Matt 28:18–20 for who has received authority to rule and what that means to believers.

Prayer Prompt: What means the most to you out of today's reading of Dan 7:15–28? What will you do about it now?

DAN 8:1–14

1. The Bible tells of many dreams. Which Bible dream do you remember the most? Why?

2. Read or listen to Dan 8:1–14. When in Daniel's life did he see this vision? Where was he? How is this introduction different from the one in Dan 7:1? Look also in Dan 7 for the meaning of animals as a symbol (Dan 7:17) and of horns as a symbol (Dan 7:24).

3. Read or listen to Dan 8:1–14. The word "great" will help to navigate this reading. Find the words "great" and note the words that tell how great for each "great." Look for a pattern.

4. Read or listen to Dan 8:1–14. Notice a different pattern now, how in Dan 7:1–14 and in 8:13–14 there is something that happens to halt the evil that had been growing. Compare and contrast those happenings.

5. Read or listen to Dan 8:1-14. How many years is 2300 days? How familiar are you with sanctuary terminology from the time of Moses and the Israelites in the wilderness? For the cleansing of the sanctuary look at Lev 16:29-34; Heb 9:22-24. Do you think Daniel would have been satisfied with what he knew so far in this reading?

Prayer Prompt: What means the most to you out of today's reading of Dan 8:1-14? What will you do about it now?

DAN 8:1-27

1. As a child, when you were told to wait, what did you do? Throw a tantrum? Sulk? Turn your desire into disdain? Find something else to do?

2. Read or listen to Dan 8:15-27. Review Dan 8:1-14 to remember the organizing pattern around the instances of the word "great." Notice that the four horns, after the first horn, and before the "little" horn, have no "great" attached. There is a ram "great," a one-horned goat "very great," a little horn "exceeding great," the same little horn "great even to the host of heaven," and the same little horn "magnified himself even to the prince of the host." Mark them in your Bible or on a chart.

3. Read or listen to Dan 8:15-27. Notice what Daniel did, what was the result, and how Daniel felt. Daniel had been told to wait 2300 days for the sanctuary to be cleansed or vindicated. In Dan 8:17, 19, 26, Daniel heard mention of other time frames. What do you think they mean and how did Daniel feel about it?

4. Read or listen to Dan 8:15-27. Now divide the interpretation to fit the designations of "great" as outlined above. Mark them in your Bible or on your chart and discuss.

5. Read or listen to Dan 8:15-27. The evening-morning vision of Dan 8:26 is the 2300 days of Dan 8:14. The deliverance of the sanctuary in Dan 8:14 matches the judgment of Dan 7:9-10, 26-17. This is the key that will stop the evil. What was Daniel told to do with the vision, and how did he feel about it?

Prayer Prompt: What means the most to you out of today's reading of Dan 8:15-27? What will you do about it now?

DAN 9:1-19

1. Tell someone who will listen what your prayer life is like. How often? For what? Do you use the Bible? What about the promises?

2. Read or listen to Dan 9:1-3. When did this story take place? What was Daniel consulting prior to his prayer? Compare the time periods of Dan 8:14 and Dan 9:2. Which is longer? Which did Daniel understand? Compare 2 Chr 36:18-23.

3. Read or listen to Dan 9:4-19. Notice the similarities between Dan 9:4 and Dan 9:15-19. Notice also the similarities between Dan 9:5-6 and Dan 9:10-11. Matching those parts as enclosing bookends leaves Dan 9:7-9 as the core of the prayer. Please notice the intertwining of the pronouns in these verses, God and Israel intertwined.

4. Read or listen to Dan 9:12-14. Daniel believed the disaster came on Jerusalem for a reason and that God was still in charge. What was the reason? And how did he know God was in charge?

5. Read or listen to Dan 9:4, 27. Covenant means promise. Whom did Daniel know to be a promise keeper? How do the curses of Dan 9:12-14 agree that God keeps promises? Would you be willing to pray confession in the plural? Would you be willing to quiz yourself about what part you may have had, and need to confess, in the troubles in our nation?

Prayer Prompt: What means the most to you out of today's reading of Dan 9:1-19? What will you do about it now?

DAN 9:20-27 A

1. Do you know where in the Bible the rapture is found? Talk about it with someone who will listen.

2. Read or listen to Dan 9:20-27. Get your bearings. Daniel wanted Jerusalem fixed. Read Dan 8:14, 26-27; 9:2 to get the train of Daniel's thought. It would be 2300 days way in the future, hence 2300 years (Num 14:34). Too long! Daniel studied the scrolls (2 Chr 36:21) and learned it should be only seventy years! It had been sixty-eight years already. Daniel fasted and prayed for God to do something, according to God's promise.

3. Read or listen to Dan 9:20–27. Who came to help Daniel understand? When had he already seen this person? He will answer Daniel's anxiety, but not so fast. From the 2300 days, seventy weeks will be cut off until the Messiah. From the seventy weeks, the first seven are cut off for the finishing of Jerusalem's wall. The next sixty-two weeks go up to the beginning of the Messiah, and the last week finishes the Messiah's work on earth. The beginning date set in Dan 9:25, represents hope for Jerusalem and hope for the world (Gal 4:4; Luke 3:1, 21–22; 4:16–19). Please discuss and help each other understand.

4. Read or listen to Dan 9:20–27. What evidence is here that God keeps promises?

5. Read or listen to Dan 9:20–27. There is no evidence here of a gap of many years before the last week. There is no evidence here of a rapture of the church. May we learn to trust God's promises, and Jesus's second coming as well as his first coming.

Prayer Prompt: What means the most to you out of today's reading of Dan 9:20–27? What will you do about it now?

DAN 9:20–27 B

1. What have you heard about a jubilee? Talk and listen to each other about stories of jubilee.

2. Read or listen to Dan 9:20–27. Compare Dan 9:2 with 2 Chr 36:21; Gen 2:1–3; and Lev 25:1–8, to learn the significance of seven and seventy. The people of Israel had not given the land its Sabbath years and were made to do so in one long stretch by being exiled to Babylon, seventy years, each year for a set of seven in history.

3. Read or listen to Dan 9:20–27. The Jubilee (Lev 25:9–34) was to come every fiftieth year and be a more drastic Sabbath for everyone, a setting free and forgiving of debt. We have no evidence that Israel ever kept the Jubilee. Some believe the emphasis here on sevens would indicate this will be a Jubilee Messiah (Isa 61:1–2; Luke 4:16–19).

4. Read or listen to Dan 9:20–27. Notice the strange wording of all the numbers, something like Lincoln's Gettysburg Address. Think of, name, and discuss some reasons for such lengthening.

5. Read or listen to Dan 9:20–27. The seventy years was cut off from the 2300 days. It takes some math, and in the early 1800s, lots of people

were doing the math. There was a well-documented worldwide movement toward preaching the second coming of Jesus because of these prophecies. Discuss together whether you feel joy or something else when you think of Jesus's return.

Prayer Prompt: What means the most to you out of today's reading of Dan 9:20–27? What will you do about it now?

DAN 9:20–27 C

1. Do you know of anyone who has taken "sanctuary" in a church? Discuss in your group how appropriate that would be.
2. Read or listen to Dan 9:20–27. Review, seventy weeks is cut off from 2300 days. In Dan 9:24 we got the beginning date for both times. At the end of seventy weeks the Messiah's first work would be finished on earth. At the end of 2300 days, the sanctuary would be cleansed, Dan 8:14. Sounds like two great events. Discuss what you think are their importance and the reason for their being tied together here.
3. Read or listen to Dan 9:20–27. The words of Dan 9:24–27 and Dan 8:14 have resonance with Exod 29:36–46. This is the story of Aaron's anointing and the inauguration of the daily sacrifices in Israel's sanctuary tent of meeting. Discuss what might be the significance of this connection.
4. Read or listen to Dan 9:20–27. Scan the book of Hebrews, noting especially Heb 8:1–5; 9:11–12, 22–28 to discover another sanctuary and consider what might be going on there right now.
5. Read or listen to Dan 9:20–27. Hebrew thinking would have looked back, from Dan 9 and the work of Jesus in providing the sacrifice for sin while on this earth, to Dan 8 and the work of Jesus wielding that provision for his people after returning to the heavenly sanctuary, to Dan 7 and the giving of the kingdom to his people after both other works are done. What would it take to let God do total cleansing in you, as God perceives cleansing?

Prayer Prompt: What means the most to you out of today's reading of Dan 9:20–27? What will you do about it now?

DAN 10

1. Tell of a time you got news that took your breath away or caused you nearly to faint. Then what?
2. Read or listen to Dan 10:1–21. This chapter is in three portions as were Dan 7 and Dan 8: a vision, an explanation, and a second-time explanation. Together in your group find logical divisions and create headings in this chapter.
3. Read or listen to Dan 10:1–21. Did you notice that there are at least two separate heavenly beings mentioned in Dan 10, the one who spoke to Daniel in first person and the one called Michael? "Michael" means "who is like God" and there is no one like God except God (Exod 15:9–11; Ps 35:10; Isa 44:6–7). The one like a man here could be taken as Gabriel (meaning "strong") from the previous chapters. Many believe then that Michael was the One Daniel saw in vision in Dan 10:5–9. Discuss with your group any comments you have about these heavenly guests.
4. Read or listen to Dan 10:12–13. Discuss the difference between the idea that there is no need for long prayers because God is already at work since our first ask, and the idea that perhaps Daniel's continued and repeated prayers helped in some way known only to those in the deep know about the cosmic war.
5. Read or listen to Dan 10:1–21. If there is a cosmic war, who of the supernatural beings would be on what sides? What do you make of Dan 10:1–3 for drastic measures to show which side a person is on in this cosmic war? What was Daniel mourning?

Prayer Prompt: What means the most to you out of today's reading of Dan 10:1–21? What will you do about it now?

DAN 11

1. Who in your group is most likely to read, or most likely to avoid reading, blow-by-blow records of long historical battles?
2. Read or listen to Dan 11:1–45. Daniel 11 runs on from Dan 10, because Daniel kept fainting away. They finally got him stabilized and started giving in plain speech what would come next in the world, yet the plain speech is still rather cryptic. In Dan 11:2, Persia is named along

with the fact that the next one is Greece. Next look for "do according to his will" to help decipher the following logical divisions (Dan 11:3, 13, 36). Then there is the "time of the end" (Dan 11:40) after which Michael stands up for his people (Dan 12:1). Can you match these to any others of the lists we have had of world empires? (See Appendix 3 for my version of a chart to match up the sevens in Daniel.)

3. Read or listen to Dan 11:1–45. Another way to look at the outline is to notice that after Dan 11:4, the King of the North and the King of the South are always attacking one another. This would include whoever ruled in those positions around the Mediterranean Sea, with Israel in the crossfire sometimes. Research and share who these countries or empires were through the centuries.

4. Read or listen to Dan 11:32–35. The record seems here to turn toward a spiritual war. How do these verses help or hinder your faith in the midst of war?

5. Read or listen to Dan 11:1–45. Compare Matt 24:1–51. In both these cases the inquirers found themselves distraught over time while looking at or thinking of the temple. In both cases the answerer gave a mixture of soon and later events, with no effort to distinguish between the sooner or later. In Matt 24 the lesson is "Watch and stay ready." Are you staying ready?

Prayer Prompt: What means the most to you out of today's reading of Dan 11:1–45? What will you do about it now?

DAN 11:32–38

1. Tell about a time you were forced to do something against your will. What were the consequences? How did you feel about it?

2. Read or listen to Dan 11:32–38. Make a list of the things that those who are wise and understanding will do or be. It seems like all those of understanding will fall, some of them will find purpose in their fall, to be made clean and white. To understand the "little help" for them, compare "none to help him" in Dan 11:45. Discuss.

3. Read or listen to Dan 11:28–39. Compare and contrast Dan 7:8, 25; also Rev 13:5–7. In the stages of empires or systems in their aggression against God, these readings would show the fifth of seven, after the first four kingdoms (Babylon as lion, Persia as bear, Greece as leopard,

and Rome as dreadful beast or dragon). What are the characteristics of this fifth empire, kingdom, or system?

4. Read or listen to Dan 11:37–38. This empire keeps nothing in sight to honor except himself above all, no God, no women, no ancestors or heritage. Then, oh yes, he does honor the god of force. Read Rev 13:15–17 and discuss what force might look like in systems and governments.

5. Read or listen to Dan 11:32–38. Compare Dan 12:3, which can be read as a parallelism, with the second part defining or enhancing the first. Though the reward is prominent in both parts, compare the two parts to discover what the wise will do. The wise refuse to use force in a world of force, yet they have an impact for good. Will you be one of the wise? Would it not be especially wise if we, in church systems, took care to protect each other from our own tendencies to control, coerce, and force?

Prayer Prompt: What means the most to you out of today's reading of Dan 11:32–38? What will you do about it now?

DAN 12

1. Who in your group liked math as a child? Who likes it now?

2. Read or listen to Dan 12:1–13. Compare these texts for these words: Time of trouble (Matt 24:21). Written in the book (Rev 3:5; 13:8; 22:19). Those who sleep awake (John 5:25–29).

3. Read or listen to Dan 12:1–13. Find the places in Dan 12 where Daniel is told to shut or seal the book. Compare the oath in Rev 10:5–7. Compare what happened to the open book (the book of Daniel probably) in Rev 10:1–2, 8–11. Compare also the instructions to John about the book of Revelation (Rev 1:3; 22:10).

4. Read or listen to Dan 12:1–13. Where did we see earlier a "man clothed in linen" (Dan 10:5–6)? Notice that Daniel is still saying he does not understand (Dan 12:8). I wonder if he felt discouraged at the words of Dan 12:10. What do you think?

5. Read or listen to Dan 12:1–13. Check out the math in Dan 12:11–13. Some say the 1335 days back up from the end of the 2300 days, like this: 1843–44 CE minus 1335 equals 508 CE (oppression begun to be set up) plus 1290 equals 1798 CE (oppression finished) minus 1260

equals 538 CE (oppression fully set up). These are great dates to keep in mind when reading Revelation about the three and one-half years, the forty-two months, and the 1260 days. What is your next step after reading Daniel?

Prayer Prompt: What means the most to you out of today's reading of Dan 12:1–13? What will you do about it now?

DAN 12:1-10

1. What will you and your group do next now that you are coming to the end of this study course?
2. Read or listen to Dan 12:1–10. Consider and tell the stories of what happened at these openings of sealed or long-lost books in Bible history: Josiah (2 Kgs 22:1–20); Esther's king (Esth 6:1–14); Ezra (Neh 8:1–12).
3. Read or listen to Dan 12:1–10. Consider and compare the book openings in courtroom settings, Rev 5:1–14; Dan 7:10, Rev 20:12. Compare and contrast the settings and the results. Discuss.
4. Read or listen to Dan 12:1–10. Jesus is the one who opens things. Read about these opened things: Rev 3:7–8; 4:1; 11:19; 12:16; 15:5; 19:11. Make a chart with columns. For each of these openings, record the (1) reference, (2) what was opened, (3) who opened it, (4) who went through or was invited through, (5) what was seen, (6) what came out, and (7) what were some results.
5. Read or listen to Dan 12:1–10. There is one thing Jesus does not open. Read Rev 3:20, and draw a picture, sing a song, or make a poem about this thing he does not open. Why do you think he does not open it? What would happen if someone did open it? The opening could picture an individual's invitation to Jesus or a whole group or society opening up to him. Jesus stands outside when shut out, knocking, non-anxious, non-coercive, present.

Prayer Prompt: What means the most to you out of today's reading of Dan 12:1–10? What will you do about it now?

Appendix 1

VERBAL PARALLELS BETWEEN DANIEL AND REVELATION, PAGE 1

Daniel		Revelation	
1:12 1:14	Prove thy servants, I beseech thee, ten days consented to them in this matter, and proved them ten days	2:10	ye may be tried; and ye shall have tribulation ten days
2:29	what should/shall come to pass hereafter (also in 2:45)	1:19	things which shall/must be hereafter (also in 4:1)
2:12	reveal, revealed, revealeth, revealer (also in 2:22,28,29,30,47; 10:1)	1:1	The Revelation of Jesus Christ
2:34	the wind carried them away, that no place was found for them	20:11	the earth and the heaven fled away; and there was found no place for them
3:25	Lo I see four men loose, walking in the midst of the fire	5:6	And I beheld, and, lo, in the midst of the throne and of the four beasts, and in the midst of the elders, stood
4:34	I praised and honoured him that liveth for ever	4:9	beasts give glory and honor and thanks to him . . . who liveth for ever and ever (see also 5:13; 7:12)
5:22 5:23	hast not humbled thine heart thou hast praised the gods of silver, and gold, of brass, iron, wood, and stone, which see not, nor hear, nor know (see also 2:32-34)	9:20	repented not . . . that they should not worship devils, and idols of gold, and silver, and brass, and stone, and of wood: which neither can see, nor hear, nor walk

VERBAL PARALLELS BETWEEN DANIEL AND REVELATION, PAGE 2

Daniel		Revelation	
6:5	We shall not find any occasion against this Daniel, except we find it against him concerning the law of his God	14:5 14:12	And in their mouth was found no guile Here are they that keep the commandments of God
7:13	behold, one like the Son of man came with the clouds of heaven	14:14	behold a white cloud, and upon the cloud one sat like unto the Son of man
7:3-21	And four great beasts came up from the sea. . . . The first was like a lion . . . a second, like a bear . . . another, like a leopard. . . . After this . . . a fourth. . . . It had ten horns . . . and a mouth speaking great things. . . . And there was given him dominion . . . that all people, nations, and languages, should serve him: his dominion is an everlasting dominion. . . . The same horn made war with the saints, and prevailed against them	13:1-7	and saw a beast rise up out of the sea, having seven heads and ten horns. . . . And the beast which I saw was like unto a leopard . . . a bear . . . a lion. . . . And there was given unto him a mouth speaking great things. . . . And it was given unto him to make war with the saints, and to overcome them . . . and power was given him over all [people], kindreds, and tongues, and nations
7:25	until a time and times and the dividing of time (also in 12:7)	12:14	for a time, and times, and half a time
8:10	even to the host of heaven; and it cast down some of the host and of the stars to the ground, and stamped upon them	12:4	his tail drew a third part of the stars of heaven and did cast them to the earth
12:4,9	But thou, O Daniel, shut up the words, and seal the book, even to the time of the end	22:7,10	Seal not the sayings of the prophecy of this book: for the time is at hand

Appendix 2

SCENE AND THEME PARALLELS BETWEEN DANIEL AND REVELATION, PAGE 1

	Daniel	Revelation
1.	Young exile in the palace (1:1-4). Jerusalem taken by Babylon (1:1-4). Temple destroyed, vessels taken as booty (1:1-4). King intended to give wisdom; God gave it instead (1:4,17). Proved ten days (1:12-14).	Aged exile on Patmos (1:9). Jerusalem taken by Rome. Temple destroyed, vessels taken as booty. Emperor intended isolation; God empowered witness (1:9-10). Tried ten days (2:10).
2.	God knew the future (2:28). Showed the future to the king (2:28). Promise of God's kingdom (2:44). Revealed the hereafter (2:28-29).	God knew the works of the churches (2-3). Showed the needed remedies (2-3). Promises to overcomer (2-3). Revealed the hereafter (1:1,19).
3.	Attempt to discover unworthy officials (3:1-8). People, nations, and languages (3:4,7,29,31). Fall down and worship golden image (3:5,6,7,10,11,15). Fire nearby in furnace (3:6, etc.). Divinity delivered by entering the flames (3:25). Four men in the midst of the fire (3:25). Out of the fire, no smell on their coats (3:26-27). King decreed worship of true God (3:29).	Search, but no one found worthy (5:2-4). Tongue, and people, and nation (5:9; 7:9). Fall down and worship Him who lives forever (4:10; 5:14). Fire burning before the throne (4:5). Lamb redeemed by entering death (5:9). Lamb in the midst of the throne (5:6). Out of tribulation, washed their robes (7:14). Lamb declared worthy of worship (5:12).
4.	Show the signs that God had wrought (4:2-3). Watcher coming down cried aloud (4:13-14). Hew down the tree (4:14). Leave stump banded (4:15). Seven years of insanity (4:25). Kingdom preserved (4:26). Lifted up his eyes (4:34). Honored Him who lives forever (4:34). Praised the King of Heaven (4:37).	Sun, moon, stars (signs Luke 21:25) (6:12-13; also 12:1). Angel coming up cried with loud voice (7:2). Hurt not the trees (7:3). Till servants sealed (7:3-4). Seven stages of book opening (6:1, etc.). Servants of God sealed (7:3-4). Wipe away tears from eyes (7:17). Glory to Him who lives forever (5:13; 7:12). Serve Him who sits on the throne (7:15).

SCENE AND THEME PARALLELS BETWEEN DANIEL AND REVELATION, PAGE 2

	Daniel	Revelation
5.	Babylon dwellers celebrated just before judgment (5:1,30). Defiled temple vessels (5:3). Praised their gods of gold (5:4). God sent warning (5:5). Hand wrote (5:5). Prophet absent but brought (5:11-13). All people, nations, and languages (5:19). King had not humbled heart (5:22). God has measured your kingdom (5:26). God has finished it (5:26).	Earth dwellers celebrated just before judgment (11:10). Destroyed the candlesticks (11:3,4,7). Worshiped idols of gold (9:20). God sent plagues (9:20). Lifted up his hand (10:5). Prophets killed but raised (11:7,11). Many peoples, nations, tongues (10:11; 11:9). Humans repented not (9:20). Measure the temple (11:1). Mystery of God finished (10:7).
6.	Last end of Daniel's life (6:1-2). Could find no occasion against him except regarding the law of God (6:5). Jealous men obtained decree (6:3-9). Lions' mouths shut (6:18,22). Daniel delivered from lions (6:18-22). Angel protected Daniel (6:22). He believed in his God (6:23). Accusers cast in (6:24; also 3:8). Prophet vindicated (6:28).	Last end of earth's history (12:17). Without fault before the throne (14:5). Keep the commandments of God (12:17; 14:12). Jealous devil made war (12:17). Serpent's mouth spewed water, earth's mouth opened (12:15-16). Child caught up from dragon (12:5). Angel announced judgment (14:6-7). Keep faith of Jesus (14:12; also 13:10). Devil cast down (12:9-10). Law and prophecy vindicated (12:17).
7.	God sat in judgment (7:10). Opened the books (7:10). Lion, bear, leopard beasts from the sea (7:3-6). Beast warred against saints (7:21). Change God's laws (7:25). Until a time, times, dividing of time (7:25).	God's judgment announced (14:7). Book of life (13:8). Lion, bear, leopard beast from the sea (13:1-2). Satan warred against remnant (12:17). Against God's commandments (12:17). For a time, times, and half a time (12:14).
8.	Some of the stars of heaven cast to the ground (8:10). Truth and sanctuary trampled (8:13). Sanctuary to be vindicated at specific time (8:14). Trampler broken without hand (8:25).	A third part of the stars of heaven cast to earth (12:4). Grapes, evil harvest trodden (14:20; see also 19:15). God's judgment announced for specific hour (14:7). Overcame by word and blood (12:11).

SCENE AND THEME PARALLELS BETWEEN DANIEL AND REVELATION, PAGE 3

	Daniel	Revelation
9.	Daniel prayed, mentioning the law of Moses (9:13). Deliverance from Egypt (9:15). Desolate sanctuary (9:17). Angel brought long-awaited explanation (9:22-23). Seventy weeks to finish (9:24). Messiah's coming (9:25). Flood (9:26). War (9:26).	Saints sang the song of Moses and the Lamb (15:3). Angels brought plagues (15:6). Temple closed in smoke (15:8). Plagues are long-awaited avenging (15:5-7; 5:8). Seventh plague, It is done (16:17). Jesus announced His coming (16:15). Great hail (16:21). Gathering for battle (16:14).
10.	Mourning over the vision (10:2). Prophet invited to understand (10:11). Quest for understanding (10:12,14). Daniel's prayer was heard (10:12). Confrontation with a worldly prince (10:13).	Mourning over Babylon (18:7,8,11,15,19; also 21:4). Prophet invited to see (17:1). Mind with wisdom (17:9). Martyrs' prayers were heard (18:20,24; 6:10; 19:2). Separation from a fallen queen (18:4,7).
11.	War and battles detailed (11:1-45). To try them [as by fire] (11:35; see also 12:10). God's people made white (11:35). Came to end, none to help (11:45).	War and battle details (19:19; 20:8-9; 16:14). Lake of fire (19:20-21; 20:10). Lamb's armies arrayed in white (19:14; 20:4). Beast, false prophet, devil in lake of fire, remnant slain (19:20-21; 20:10).
12.	Michael stands for His people (12:1). Delivered if written in the book (12:1). Turn many to righteousness (12:3). Shine forever (12:3). Seal the book till the time of the end (12:4,9). All these things shall be finished (12:7). Oath over the waters of the river (12:7).	God dwells with His people (21:3). Enter if written in the book (21:27). Hear and give invitation, Come (22:17). Reign forever (22:5). Seal not the book for the time is at hand (22:7,10). It is done (21:6). Promise of fountain of water of life (21:6).

Appendix 3

SEVENS IN DANIEL

Metal Image Dan 2	Wild Animals Dan 7	Domestic Animals Dan 8	Great War Dan 11
Head Gold Babylon	Lion Eagle's Wings	(None)	(None)
Chest Silver Persia	Bear Raised One Side (5)	Ram "Great" (4) Persia "Do according to his will" (4)	Four More Kings in Persia Stir Up Against Greece (2)
Thighs Brass Greece	Leopard Wings, 4 Heads (6)	Goat, 4 Horns "Very Great" (8) Greece	Mighty King "Do according to his will" (3–15)
Legs Iron Rome	Dreadful Animal Iron Teeth, Ten Horns (7)	Little Horn "Exceeding Great" (9)	King of the North "Do according to his will" (16–27)
Feet Iron & Clay Partly strong, partly weak	Little Horn "Against the Most High" (8, 25)	Little Horn "Great Even to the Host of Heaven" (10)	King of the North "Do" (28–35) Someone else will "Do" (32)
Mingle, Not Mix Stone Cut Out	Judgment Scene (26)	Vindication of Sanctuary "Even Against the Prince of the Host" (11)	King of the North "Do according to his will" (36–39)
Stone Set Up Filled the Earth	Kingdom Given to the Saints (27)	Little Horn Destroyed "Broken without hand" (25)	Time of the End "Come to his end with none to help him" (40–43)

Bibliography

Aland, Kurt, et al., eds. *The Greek New Testament*. New York: United Bible Societies, 1975.
Anonymous. *The Pearl Poet*. Translated and Introduction by Margaret Williams. New York: Random House, 1967.
Augsburger, David. *Caring Enough to Confront: How to Understand and Express Your Deepest Feelings Toward Others*. Ventura, CA: Regal, 1981.
———. *Caring Enough to Forgive: True Forgiveness and Caring Enough to Not Forgive: False Forgiveness*. Ventura, CA: Regal, 1981.
———. *Caring Enough to Hear and Be Heard*. Scottdale, PA: Herald, 1982.
Beale, G. K. *The Book of Revelation: A Commentary on the Greek Text*. The New International Greek Testament Commentary. Edited by I. Howard Marshall and Donald A. Hagner. Grand Rapids, MI: Eerdmans, 1999.
———. *John's Use of the Old Testament in Revelation*. Library of New Testament Studies. Edited by Stanley E. Porter. New York: Bloomsbury T. & T. Clark, 1998.
———. *The Use of Daniel in Jewish Apocalyptic Literature and in the Revelation of St. John*. Eugene, OR: Wipf & Stock, 1984.
"Bible Societies." https://www.encyclopedia.com/philosophy-and-religion/christianity/protestant-denominations/bible-societies.
Boring, M. Eugene. *Revelation*. Interpretation: A Bible Commentary for Teaching and Preaching. Edited by James Luther Mays et al. Louisville, KY: John Knox, 1989.
Bowman, Cyril. *Christianity: The East/West Divide*. N.p.: n.p., 2002.
Brueggemann, Walter. *The Bible Makes Sense*. Rev. ed. Louisville, KY: Westminster John Knox, 2001.
———. *The Prophetic Imagination*. 2nd ed. Minneapolis, MN: Fortress, 2001.
Collins, Adela Yarbro. *The Apocalypse*. New Testament Message 22. Edited by Wilfrid Harrington, OP, and Donald Senior, CP. Wilmington, DE: Glazier, 1979.
Collins, John J. *The Apocalyptic Imagination: An Introduction to Jewish Apocalyptic Literature*. 3rd ed. Grand Rapids, MI: Eerdmans, 2016.
Cook, Jerry, with Stanley C. Baldwin. *Love, Acceptance and Forgiveness: Equipping the Church to Be Truly Christian in a Non-Christian World*. Ventura, CA: Regal, 1979.
Craddock, Fred B. *Overhearing the Gospel*. Rev. ed. St. Louis, MO: Chalice, 2002.
Curtis, A. Kenneth, et al. *The 100 Most Important Events in Christian History*. Grand Rapids, MI: Revel, 1991.
D'Aubigne, Jean Henri Merle. *History of the Reformation of the Sixteenth Century*. 5 vols. New York: Carter, 1857.

De Tocqueville, Alexis. Translated by John Bonner. 1856. Reprint, *The Old Regime and the Revolution*. Eastford, CT: Martino Fine, 2017.

Doukhan, Jacques B. *Secrets of Daniel: Wisdom and Dreams of a Jewish Prince in Exile*. Hagerstown, MD: Review and Herald, 2000.

———. *Secrets of Revelation: The Apocalypse Through Hebrew Eyes*. Hagerstown, MD: Review and Herald, 2002.

Edwards, Mark, Jr. "Apocalypticism Explained: Martin Luther." *PBS Frontline*, n.d. https://www.pbs.org/wgbh/pages/frontline/shows/apocalypse/explanation/martinluther.html.

Elgin, Suzette Haden. *The Gentle Art of Verbal Self-Defense*. New York: Barnes & Noble, 1980.

Emmerson, Richard K., and Bernard McGinn, eds. *The Apocalypse in the Middle Ages*. Ithaca, NY: Cornell University Press, 1992.

Evans, Patricia. *Controlling People: How to Recognize, Understand, and Deal with People Who Try to Control You*. Avon, MA: Adams Media, 2002.

———. *The Verbally Abusive Relationship: How to Recognize It and How to Respond*. Holbrook, MA: Adams Media Corporation, 1996.

Fiorenza, Elisabeth Schussler. *The Book of Revelation: Justice and Judgment*. Philadelphia, PA: Fortress, 1985.

———. *Revelation*. Proclamation Commentaries. Edited by Gerhard Krodel. Minneapolis, MN: Fortress, 1991.

"Founding Dates of States, Colleges, and Universities in America by Region." https://mwolverine.com/Founding_Dates_States_Colleges.html.

Friedman, Edwin H. *A Failure of Nerve: Leadership in the Age of the Quick Fix*. 1999. Reprint, New York: Seabury, 2007.

———. *Generation to Generation: Family Process in Church and Synagogue*. New York: Guilford, 1985.

Goulston, Mark. *Just Listen: Discover the Secret to Getting Through to Absolutely Anyone*. New York: American Management Association, 2010.

Hamm, Richard L. *Recreating the Church: Leadership for the Postmodern Age*. St. Louis, MO: Chalice, 2007.

Haugk, Kenneth C. *Antagonists in the Church: How to Identify and Deal with Destructive Conflict*. Minneapolis, MN: Augsburg, 1988.

Hayes, John H., and Carl R. Holladay. *Biblical Exegesis: A Beginner's Handbook*. 3rd ed. Louisville, KY: Westminster John Knox, 2007.

Jenkins, Philip. *The Lost History of Christianity: The Thousand-Year Golden Age of the Church in the Middle East, Africa, and Asia—and How It Died*. New York: Harper Collins, 2008.

Koester, Craig R. *Revelation and the End of All Things*. Grand Rapids, MI: Eerdmans, 2001.

Kung, Hans. *The Catholic Church: A Short History*. Translated by John Bowden. 2001. Reprint, New York: Random House, 2003.

Lynch, Joseph H. *The Medieval Church: A Brief History*. New York: Longman, 1992.

Maxwell-Stuart, P. G. *Chronicle of the Popes: The Reign-by-Reign Record of the Papacy from St. Peter to the Present*. New York: Thames and Hudson, 1997.

Paulien, Jon. *The Deep Things of God: An Insider's Guide to the Book of Revelation*. Hagerstown, MD: Review and Herald, 2004.

———. *The Gospel from Patmos: Everyday Insights for Living from the Last Book of the Bible.* Hagerstown, MD: Review and Herald, 2007.

Peterson, Eugene H. *Reversed Thunder: The Revelation of John & the Praying Imagination.* San Francisco, CA: Harper, 1988.

Reis, Andre. *Echoes of the Most Holy: The Day of Atonement in the Book of Revelation.* Eugene, OR: Wipf & Stock, 2022.

Richard, Pablo. *Apocalypse: A People's Commentary on the Book of Revelation.* Eugene, OR: Wipf & Stock, 1995.

Rowland, Christopher. *Radical Christianity: A Reading of Recovery.* Eugene, OR: Wipf & Stock, 1988.

Schwab, Klaus, and Thierry Malleret. *The Great Narrative: For a Better Future.* Switzerland; Forum, 2022.

The Septuagint with Apocrypha: Greek and English. Translated into English by Sir Lancelot C. L. Brenton. London: Bagster, 1851.

Sivaramamurti, Calambur, and Carole Straw. "St. Gregory the Great." https://www.britannica.com/biography/St-Gregory-the-Great.

Stefanovic, Ranko. *Plain Revelation: A Reader's Introduction to the Apocalypse.* Berrien Springs, MI: Andrews University Press, 2013.

———. *Revelation of Jesus Christ: Commentary on the Book of Revelation.* 2nd ed. Berrien Springs, MI: Andrews University Press, 2009.

Stefanovic, Zdravko. *Daniel, Wisdom to the Wise: Commentary on the Book of Daniel.* Nampa, ID: Pacific, 2007.

Tonstad, Sigve K. *Revelation.* Paideia Commentaries on the New Testament. Edited by Mikeal C. Parsons et al. Grand Rapids, MI: Baker Academic, 2019.

Tomkins, Stephen. *A Short History of Christianity.* Grand Rapids, MI: Eerdmans, 2005.

Tucker, Mike. *Meeting Jesus in the Book of Revelation: Taking the Fear Out of the Bible's Scariest Book.* Nampa, ID: Pacific, 2007.

United Nations. "Transforming Our World: The 2030 Agenda for Sustainable Development." https://sdgs.un.org/2030agenda.

Vetne, Reimar. *Jesus in the Book of Revelation.* Ulefoss, Norway: Bibloy, 2016.

Wainwright, Arthur W. *Mysterious Apocalypse: Interpreting the Book of Revelation.* Eugene, OR: Wipf & Stock, 1993.

Walker, Williston. *A History of the Christian Church.* Revised by Robert T. Handy. 3rd ed. New York: Scribner's, 1970.

Wengst, Klaus. *Pax Romana and the Peace of Jesus Christ.* Translated by John Bowden. Philadelphia: Fortress, 1987.

White, Ellen G. *The Great Controversy Between Christ and Satan: As Revealed in the Lives and Struggles of God's People from Christ's Time Down Through the Centuries to Our Time and Beyond.* Mountain View, CA: Pacific, 1950.

Wilson, Mark W. *Revelation.* Zondervan Illustrated Bible Backgrounds Commentary. Edited by Clinton E. Arnold. Grand Rapids, MI: Zondervan, 2002.

Zalabak, Wilma. "Toward 'Diversity in Cooperation': A Response to Blazen, Larson, and Mashchak." *Adventist Today* 4.1 (1996) 14–15.

Index

Abyss, Bottomless Pit, 67–68, 109
Adventure, 1, 4, 44, 51, 78–79, 86
Air, 34, 53, 82, 108–9, 115, 132
Anxiety, 44, 47, 50, 75, 78, 162, 167

Blasphemy, 57, 67–68, 72, 83, 91, 123, 125, 138–39
Bully, 47, 156–57
Business, 44, 49–50, 79, 100–101

Character of God, 74, 76, 140
Chiasm, 38–39, 59
Communication, 4, 10, 46–48, 62, 84, 136
Conflict, 40, 44, 47
Consumption, 47, 77–78, 139

Deductive, 1–3, 7, 10–11
Diversity, 1n, 46–47, 57, 82

Fear, Shame, and Guilt, 10, 40, 44, 47, 74–79, 83, 85–86
Figures of Speech, 3, 65
Forest, Trees, 53, 102, 106
Futurist, 2, 10, 44

God Can, I Cannot, and I Decide to Let Him, 62, 85

Historicist, 2, 35, 43–45, 49, 52, ,55, 60, 70–71, 73, 79

"I" Language, Saying "I", 46–47
Imagination, 1, 3, 7, 8–9, 36–38, 44, 55, 72, 84, 86

Justice, 51, 64, 116, 137, 149

Life Cycle, 48–51, 84, 100–101, 106, 115, 135
Listening, 46–47, 80, 90, 101, 124
Love, Acceptance, and Forgiveness, 10, 44, 72n, 76–79, 86

Metaphor, 3, 65, 93, 97, 145

Nature, 51–52, 59, 84–85, 155

Parable, 3, 25, 65, 71
Parallel, 1n, 29–30, 37–39, 54–55
Preterist, 2, 8, 10, 43–44
Production, 47, 77–78
Project, 10, 44, 49, 78, 84, 98–101, 106–7, 115, 123

Sabbath, 17, 61–62, 83, 110–11, 115, 162
Sea, Ocean, 53, 60–61, 63–64, 68, 78, 82, 84, 102, 107, 109, 125, 132–33, 144
Sustainable, 59–60n
Symbol, 1–4, 11, 65–66, 91, 131, 138, 158–59

Ten Commandments, 40, 60, 82–83, 110–11, 121

Verbal Abuse, 47

Warfare, 53–54
Water, Fresh, Drinking, 53, 63–64, 108, 115, 132–33
Wealth, 20–21, 72, 79

www.ingramcontent.com/pod-product-compliance
Lightning Source LLC
Chambersburg PA
CBHW051928160426
43198CB00012B/2078